T0324041

Aki-wayn-zih

McGill-Queen's Indigenous and Northern Studies
(In memory of Bruce G. Trigger)

JOHN BORROWS, SARAH CARTER, AND ARTHUR J. RAY, EDITORS

The McGill-Queen's Indigenous and Northern Studies series publishes books about Indigenous peoples in all parts of the northern world. It includes original scholarship on their histories, archaeology, laws, cultures, governance, and traditions. Works in the series also explore the history and geography of the North, where travel, the natural environment, and the relationship to land continue to shape life in particular and important ways. Its mandate is to advance understanding of the political, legal, and social relations between Indigenous and non-Indigenous peoples, of the contemporary issues that Indigenous peoples face as a result of environmental and economic change, and of social justice, including the work of reconciliation in Canada. To provide a global perspective, the series welcomes books on regions and communities from across the Arctic and Subarctic circumpolar zones.

Aki-wayn-zih

A Person as Worthy as the Earth

ELI BAXTER

Edited by Matthew Ryan Smith

McGill-Queen's University Press

Montreal & Kingston • London • Chicago

ISBN 978-0-2280-0807-1 (cloth)
ISBN 978-0-2280-0922-1 (ePDF)
ISBN 978-0-2280-0923-8 (ePUB)

Legal deposit third quarter 2021
Bibliothèque nationale du Québec

Printed in Canada on acid-free paper that is 100% ancient forest free
(100% post-consumer recycled), processed chlorine free

This book has been published with the help of a grant from the
Canadian Federation for the Humanities and Social Sciences,
through the Awards to Scholarly Publications Program, using funds
provided by the Social Sciences and Humanities Research Council
of Canada.

Funded by the Government of Canada   Financé par le gouvernement du Canada   Canada   Canada Council for the Arts   Conseil des arts du Canada

We acknowledge the support of the Canada Council for the Arts.

Nous remercions le Conseil des arts du Canada de son soutien.

Library and Archives Canada Cataloguing in Publication

Title: Aki-wayn-zih : a person as worthy as the Earth / Eli Baxter ;
   edited by Matthew Ryan Smith.
Names: Baxter, Eli, author. | Smith, Matthew Ryan, 1983- editor.
Description: Series statement: McGill-Queen's Indigenous and
   northern studies ; 102 | Includes bibliographical references and
   index. | Text in English. Includes some text in Anishinaabay
   with English translation.
Identifiers: Canadiana (print) 20210215801 | Canadiana (ebook)
   2021021791X | ISBN 9780228008071 (hardcover) | ISBN
   9780228009221 (pdf) | ISBN 9780228009238 (EPUB)
Subjects: LCSH: Baxter, Eli. | LCSH: Indigenous peoples—Ontario,
   Northern—Social life and customs. | LCSH: Indigenous peoples—
   Ontario, Northern—History. | LCSH: Indigenous peoples—
   Ontario, Northern—Social conditions. | LCSH: Indigenous
   peoples—Ontario, Northern—Biography. | CSH: Indigenous
   peoples—Ontario, Northern—Residential schools. | LCGFT:
   Autobiographies.
Classification: LCC E99.C6 B39 2021 | DDC 305.897/33307131092—dc23

For my parents, Gilbert-iban and Barbara-iban;
my family, Elizabeth, Quinn, and Rachel;
and to all residential school survivors.

Contents

Figures

All photos by the author.

Aki-wayn-zih

Prologue

"Ni-wee-i-zha kay-neen!"

("I want to go, too!")

This was my request and desire to go to residential school. It came from the fact that I could not count from one to ten in English. My first language is Ojibway.

My older brother and sisters came back from residential school every summer. Our older cousins went as well. They were taught English there and could easily count from one to ten.

That summer we played hide-and-seek in the bush by the river. During the game I would get caught and have to count from one to ten while the others hid. They would not let me count in Ojibway, so my father had to count for me in English. I didn't like that much.

When we returned home that evening to eat, I told my parents that I wanted to go to residential school so I could count from one to ten in English like my siblings and cousins. I remember the look on their faces. I was probably the only Anishinaabay person that actually wanted to go to residential school.

PART ONE

Anishinaabay Kih-kayn-daa-soh-win
(Anishinaabay Knowledge)

Ningiinihtaawig Pihnaakohgiisis Niizhitana niswih,
  Midaaswih-zhaangaswih naanihmihtahnah-niiwin.
(I was born 23 October 1954.)
Ningiinihtaawig wetih noopihmiing; Kihcih Ziibiing, Washi
  Sahgeguniing.
(I was born over there in the wilderness; on the Albany River,
  on Washi Lake.)
Kahnihtaawihgihyaan niswih mangoog kiipohniiwug
  sahgeguniing.
(When I was born three loons landed on the lake.)
Ningiibiinihgoog wetih manitokaaning; giipohniiwug cih
  kihkendumohwaach egiitahgohsihniiyaan.
(They brought me from the spirit world; they landed to know
  if I arrived.)
Ningiiohmbihgii nohpihmiing. Anishinaabemowin eta
  ningiinoondaan.
(I grew up in the wilderness. The Anishinaabay language
  was the only thing I heard.)
Ningiibihmaatis andahwegihgewin aiitush mahwongiigewin
  bihmaatisihwin.
(I lived the hunting and gathering society.)

Pah-goh-nah-gii-sis (Hole in the Sky).
Change comes into the lives of the Anishinaabayg.

CHAPTER 1

Introduction

Booz-hoo.
Eli Baxter nin-dih-zhin-nih-kaaz.
A-goh-keeng nin-doon-jih-baa.
At-tick nih-do-daym.

This is the traditional way of introducing yourself in Ojibway. You say "booz-hoo" to people to find out if they are Na-na-boo-zhoo. Na-na-boo-zhoo is the spirit who used to live with our people. He is also a trickster and a magician. He left us long ago and we are still looking for him. We know that he is still around some-where and that is why we ask people if he or she is Nanaboozhoo. Many people say we got the word "booz-hoo" from the French term "bonjour," meaning "hello"; we say the French got the word from us.

"Eli Baxter nin-dih-zhin-nih-kaaz" translates to "Eli Baxter is my name" in English. I did not use my Anishinaabay ceremonial name because I did not receive one from my parents. My siblings and I did not get our names in the naming ceremony we were sup-posed to have when we were infants. Our parents did this for our own protection. They did not want us to use any Anishinaabay ceremonies when we went to residential school because we could be punished. It was left to us to get our names when we became adults. I still haven't got around to it yet. It is said that you can't enter into the spirit world when it is time for you to go – you need to have your Anishinaabay name or they won't recognize you.

"A-goh-keeng nin-doon-jih-baa" means "I am from Ogoki Post." Ogoki Post is a reserve community in Northern Ontario. It is situated on the shores of the Albany River, which flows from Lake St Joseph into James Bay. Our people call it Kih-chi Zii-bii, or "Big River." This river was one of the main waterways used by the Hudson's Bay Company as their trading route. At the mouth of the river live the Mush-kee-goog, the People of the Swamp. The Cree have lived here since the time when the ice left from the last ice age. I am saying "Wa-chi-yay! Wa-chi-yay!" (Hello! Hello!) to them. We are one of the most northern Ojibway nations. The other community is Eabametoong, also called Fort Hope, which is further up the river than we are. The headwater for the Albany River is in the area known as Sioux Lookout.

"At-tick nih-do-daym" means "My Clan is the Caribou." We follow our father's Clan. The Caribou Clan belongs to the Hoof family of Clans, meaning that we are also related to the Deer, Elk, and Bison Clans. We consider our Clans as family.

The Anishinaabay introduction is used to tell people our names, where we are from, and what our Clan is. Telling people where you are from also informs them of your personal history and your people's history. It also tells those you meet the spirit protectors of where you're from. Your Clan tells them what kind of responsibilities you have within your community; for example, if you are from the Hoof family of Clans, like I am, you are seen by others as being gentle and kind, like the deer or caribou. Traditionally, we are the poets and peacemakers because we choose our words carefully and seek to avoid violence. There are seven original Clans: Crane, Loon, Fish, Bear, Marten, Caribou, and Bird. Each one has its own character and role in the community.

This is the traditional introduction of the Anishinaabayg, the People. At the present time, it is used only by fluent speakers of the Anishinaabay language when talking to other fluent speakers. The language we heard was the traditional language used by our parents, who were taught by their parents. It is the language that was used by only the Anishinaabayg. The language spoken before European contact was still being used by our parents and our grandparents. Many of our grandparents did not speak a word of English. Our parents had limited command of the English language. My generation, here on Turtle Island, are the last of the hunting and gathering society. We are the last speakers.

When was the last time you had a dream in the Anishinaabay language?

CHAPTER 2

O-way nih-ta-tih-bah-chi-moh-win-naan
(Our story)

This is our story (o-way nih-ta-tih-bah-chi-moh-win-naan).

The Anishinaabay Kih-kayn-daa-soh-win (Anishinaabay Knowledge) is entirely in our language. As such, the Anishinaabay education system is already in our language. The history, science, math, education, philosophy, and spiritual teachings are in our language. In our languages there is also the Anishinaabay Pah-gittin-nih-gay-win-nun (the Anishinaabay Laws). These laws are sacred, and they supersede any European law. In order to bring back our Kih-kayn-daa-soh-win we need to learn from the past in the present so we can benefit in the future.

What was our Anishinaabay Kih-kayn-daa-soh-win before European contact? The Anishinaabay Kih-kayn-daa-soh-win is still being used today but it flourished here on Turtle Island before European contact. At that time, our education system produced no jails because we had a strong justice system. A person was excommunicated by the village and nation by sending them out to live in the wilderness alone with no contact to anyone. The elders were looked after by the youngest sibling. Our education system had us live to be three hundred years old. We have oral history passed down from our ancestors where people used to observe Halley's Comet three times during their lifetime.

A person gets this title when he or she knows as much knowledge as the earth. They know the secrets of the earth and the universe. Their knowledge is in the language. They know the Anishinaabay Creation Story. They can recite it from the beginning to the end. To do so takes seven days. It is the knowledge of where creation started and how the earth began. It talks about the spiritual world and the physical world. All living and non-living things on the planet are named in the language. It identifies the universe: the stars, moon, and sun, the other planets, and even other worlds. It teaches us about Kizhay Manitou (the Kind Spirit) and all the other spirits that are on the land, in the water, and in the air.

"Aki-wayn-zih" means "a person who is as worthy as the earth." Because Aki-wayn-zih know as much as the earth and know how to heal themselves just like the earth can, they are given that respected title. Our Anishinaabay education system teaches our children to reach the level of being an Aki-wayn-zih.

The Anishinaabay language is a language of instruction. It was passed on orally from one generation to the other, then to others. The language was heard by infant children in the wigwams (dome-shaped houses). The grandparents, parents, aunts and uncles, cousins, and brothers and sisters were present to pass on the language. Visitors from the village were also involved as they came to the wigwam to view the children. The children were also allowed to hear the Chief and Council speak and were included in special community ceremonies. Our language includes stories, songs, everyday conversations, and prayers. It teaches and it is taught.

Every wigwam with children inside included speakers of different ages with different levels of knowledge and fluency. The infants would listen to them and were encouraged to imitate the younger speakers. The younger speakers wanted to speak better so they listened and saw how their parents and older siblings interacted. Although the parents spoke with great skill, the best speakers were the storytellers. Every village had several storytellers. Every family had a person who was able to tell the stories of the family, the village, the history of the Anishinaabayg, and the at-soh-kaan-nun (the traditional stories). Every young person in the village wanted to be a storyteller with great oratory skills.

Every Clan in the village had a storyteller. Storytellers had vast knowledge and were sought out by the Chief and Council to be representatives for the village. The storyteller had to have excellent physical traits. He had to be able to run long distances and travel alone by foot for several days. He had to be strong and powerful, and he had to have great stamina. The storyteller also had to have fine diplomatic skills with the ability to communicate important messages from his village to others. The only things he carried were his medicine pouch and the oral messages he was required to deliver. These messages often contained information that the Chief wanted the other Chiefs to hear about during the next nation gathering, or about times of trouble that needed to be addressed.

The "Song by the Edge of the Woods" was delivered by all the messengers. If the messenger did not recite the "Song by the Edge of the Woods" and simply walked into the village, anyone had the right to attack him. The dogs would be the first to let the people know there was a visitor outside. When he arrived at the village where the message was to be delivered, the messenger built a fire near the village to let the people there know that he was a visitor and wanted to come into the village. He would sing. The Chief is then notified, and he sends out a delegation to meet the stranger. By the time the delegation from the village reaches the messenger, the fire is burning, and the song is still being sung. There is no talking yet.

The delegates sit down around the fire and the messenger takes up his pipe with tobacco in it. The pipe is smoked by everyone at the fire. The messenger introduces himself to the delegation and says that he has a message for the Chief and Council. They all get up, put the fire out, and walk into the village. The messenger is then walked into the village. He greets the Chief by saying his own Anishinaabay name. This tells the Chief and everyone what his purpose in life is. He says where he is from, and this indicates his nation and the history of his place. He tells them his Clan, and this lets everyone know which Clan will feed, shelter, and protect him in this territory.

The Chief hears that there is a message from the messenger's Chief. The Chief welcomes the messenger and tells him to deliver the message to everyone at the Council meeting to be held later. The runner is given time to rest and eat while the meeting is set up and everyone is told about it. The message is told to everyone, and there is a response that the runner will take back. The runner is looked after by his Clan before he leaves. He is walked out of the village and he returns to his village.

All Anishinaabayg followed the Anishinaabay Pah-git-tin-nih-gay-win-nun, the Anishinaabay Laws. These laws come from our Clans. Our do-daym, our Clan, tells us our laws, protocols, and responsibilities. Each village had a Clan. The Clans had their own responsibilities for their village. The Bear Clan protected the village and they were also the healers. They went out to patrol the surrounding areas for any enemy that might be approaching. While they were out in the wilderness, they observed the plants and the animals and the birds. They found out the foods and medicines from knowing all about the animals' and birds' behaviour. Plant behaviour was also observed during the moon phases. They knew what plants were the most potent for different types of medicines to cure the different ailments. For instance, a certain plant, when it grows out in the open meadow, will thrive and be safe to eat; but it becomes poisonous when it grows in the forest because the sun has not purified it.

The Loon and Crane Clans were considered the chieftains. They carried their loud cries for people to listen. Their voices spoke to Kih-zhay Ma-nih-to (the Kind Creator). The other messenger was the Thunder Bird who carried the messages from the Clans to Kih-zhay Ma-nih-to and vice versa. The Loon and Crane Clans were the intellectuals. The Turtle Clan sent out the laws and messages. They are considered to be part of the Fish Clan. They told and held the laws of the Anishinaabayg. Every other Clan was told about the laws and followed them. People captured and taken prisoner in wars were placed in the Marten Clan and they were required to follow certain protocols. They were the warriors and they were the ones sent out to battle any enemy that approached the village. Each Clan was responsible for the Anishinaabay Laws and protocols. This was our governance system. Clans were like family; they offered protection, healing, and teachings, provided shelter, and gave spiritual guidance.

The Anishinaabay Kih-kayn-daa-soh-win knowledge system has several levels of learning. The first level was the infancy stage; the next was the child stage, also considered the good life stage; followed by the fast life stage; and then after that was the adult stage. The infancy level was children from birth to seven years old; the next stage was from eight years old to fourteen years old; the stage after that was from fifteen to nineteen; and the adult stage was from adulthood to the next life.

All knowledge was transferred in the Anishinaabay language. Every infant started hearing the language while in their mother's womb. Later, the language was heard inside the wigwam. Infants are believed to come from the spirit world. They picked their parents and their journey was long. The parents knew the baby needed their Anishinaabay i-zhih-nih-kaa-zoh-win (Anishinaabay name). Their Anishinaabay i-zhih-nih-kaa-zoh-win was to be given by an elder. The elders in the village knew they would be asked to name the baby and they would conduct the naming ceremony. The elder asked by the parents would be given tobacco to do the ceremony. The elder then accepts the tobacco and the parents are told to wait until a dream or a vision came about the child. The elder tells the parents when it is time to hold the naming ceremony. It is held very early in the morning, usually before sunrise. The parents prepare the feast and have gifts for the elder. Relatives and friends are invited to attend. The elder comes with other elders he has invited. There are four sponsors picked by the parents and they will provide guidance as the child grows up. Everyone sits in a circle while there are songs and prayers given by the elder. He then explains the dream or vision about the baby. The name is given with an explanation of the meaning of the name. The name tells everyone the purpose of this baby's life. The four sponsors will provide guidance for the baby as he grows. Those present are considered witnesses for the event.

From infancy to seven years old, it was the responsibility of women to teach the children. The mother, the aunts, the older women, the cousins, and the Koh-koh-mug (the grandmothers) were all teachers to the children. The children watched and heard the Anishinaabay language spoken in their daily activities. Stories, songs, and prayers are said for the children to hear and understand. The only word that was discouraged was the word "I" during this stage. The children were taught to use "we" instead. This is the reason why we don't have words for "he" or "she" in the Anishinaabay language. Shee-mayns is used to identify a younger brother or sister. It was always "we" because of the collective and cohesive nature of the group that needed to be taught.

The younger children in the village wanted to speak as well as their older siblings. The older siblings want to have a better command of the language as their parents and elders do. Yet everyone wanted to be a special orator like the storytellers. The children heard the language in the village during the summer. In the fall, winter, and the spring, nuclear families went to their traditional hunting grounds as our hunting and gathering society needed them to. The immediate family members formed the main group, along with their grandparents, and one of their uncles and his family. The men went hunting while the women looked after the wigwam along with the children.

"At-soh-kayn! At-soh-kayn!" was what the children begged just before bed during the snowy winter months. This means "tell us a story! Tell us a story!" Stories were told to every Anishinaabay child in the Anishinaabay language here on Turtle Island before European contact. Our parents still told us these stories when we were growing up. They hold the entire curriculum of the Anishinaabay Kih-kayn-daa-soh-win. These stories have history, geography, science, math, philosophy, language arts, social studies, laws, human behaviour, the universe, the constellations, and the physical and spiritual beings on earth. These stories developed our skills and memory. The young children repeated the stories to the younger children. They would even create their own spin to the stories.

There was always a family member who was a gifted storyteller. There were different people from the villages who were claimed to be great storytellers. Everyone wanted to hear their stories and they were held in high esteem. Everyone wanted to speak like them. These stories were told only when there was snow on the ground. This protocol is followed to this day. Whenever a parent or grandparent started with "Ways-kuch ..." or with "Pay-shih-koh ...," we got excited because we knew a story was about to be told. Ways-kuch means "a long time ago." Pay-shih-koh means "once."

The stories would start early in the evening and would not end until late in the night. The stories told of spiritual beings with supernatural powers that lived among us mortal beings. Some characters were able to change into human form. One of these was Nanabush, a spirit who always wanted to take the human form of an Anishinaabay. He was a magician, a jokester, and a teacher who could also change himself into animate or inanimate objects. He was always involved in many adventures with humans and animals. He was lazy, foolish, childish, energetic, and smart. He came to the human world because his grandmother, Koh-kohm, was a human being. He always wanted to help and be with his Koh-kohm. He had many names in Anishinaabay country such as Waynabozho, Nanabush, Nanabozho, Gloscap, and Wee-sah-kay-chaak.

The reason why these stories were told in the winter was that there was not really anything to do during those winter nights. Everything was frozen. The stories were so good that if they were told during the spring, there would not be any growth since everyone would be inside their wigwams listening to the stories. In summer, if everyone would be listening to the stories, no food would be looked after. In the fall, there would not be any harvesting or gathering food for the winter. That was what my mother told me.

CHAPTER 3

Pih-mah-tis-sih-win
(The stages of life)

The tih-kih-naa-gun (cradleboard) was everyone's first classroom. It was made to keep the infant safe and warm. It was always with the mother. The baby is wrapped up in a waa-bih-chee-bih-zohn, a soft warm cloth placed in a small pouch laced up with moose hide string. This pouch was often filled with dried moss which functioned as a diaper. Moss was gathered in the spring, summer, and fall. Parents went into the bush where there was plenty of moss. It was picked up and hung on the branches of spruce trees to be used later and also so that there would be moss available during the winter. This moss was used as diapers in the waa-bih-chee-bih-zohn. It was so absorbent. There was never any diaper rash. It was also biodegradable.

The cradleboard was made with flat boards connected together with moose hide string. A huge spruce tree would be cut down. It was split in half using dried wood wedges. The halves were then roughly shaved using an axe into boards. The two boards are then further shaved down using a hand-held wood shaver. They are shaved until they become thin boards. The boards are then surrounded along the outer edges with thin cedar strips. These thin walls keep the baby in place. The walls are sturdy as they are attached to the board using raw moose hide with holes drilled through the wood. The board is then covered with a cloth covering that has two sides. These two sides have loops in them to be used as tying holes to be pulled together to cover the baby that is in the waa-bih-chee-bih-zohn.

The waa-bih-chee-bih-zohn is placed inside the cradleboard. At the front part of the cradleboard, where the baby's head was going to be, there was a roll bar made out of cedar. This was to protect the baby from falling face-first onto the ground. This cedar bar was also good for the mother because she could hold it to rock the tih-kih-naa-gun back and forth when it was time for the baby to sleep. Various toys were hung from the bar so the baby can play with them. These were usually carved animals for the baby to handle and use as they were teething.

The tih-kih-naa-gun was wrapped with a beaded covering along the sides and the bottom. It was decorated with designs of images of animals, birds, and flowers. These images will be encountered later in life in the wilderness. The two sides met at the middle and the edges had small holes along the covering. They were tied together using moose hide strings. It was like tying up your moccasins. The baby inside the waa-bih-chee-bih-zohn was placed inside the cradleboard. When the tih-kih-naa-gun was laced up, the only thing showing was the baby's face. The baby would fall asleep. The cradleboard is placed on the blankets or it was leaned up against the wall of the wigwam. When the baby woke up the lacing was loosened up to the baby's chest. This was done so the baby could play with the toys and was able to move his or her arms. The babies were also fed when they were inside the cradleboard. The babies were watching and listening to all the activities that were happening all around them. They were also taken outside.

There was a thump line attached to the back of the cradleboard. This strap was placed across the chest of the person carrying the baby. The baby travelled backwards for the first part of its life. The strap was used to hang the cradleboard with the baby in it on strong branches to keep it off the ground. This also keeps the dogs and other animals away from the baby's face.

Anishinaabay babies lived in the tih-kih-naa-gun until they were ready to walk. They heard the language spoken by their immediate family. The infants heard the songs and prayers in the wigwam. Families travelled during the summer to a gathering of nations. Infants were brought along to see and hear the great orators from each village. They saw and heard the stories, the ceremonies, the pow-wows, and the speeches given by the leaders. Infants were also present when the games were played.

When the children became mobile and were able to walk and run on their own, they left the tih-kih-naa-gun. The mothers, along with their female family members, looked after the children as they started to explore the world outside. The children were allowed to explore the fields, meadows, forest, lakes, and rivers along with their older siblings. Dogs were ever-present and would alert them to danger or protect them. The children were present when there was work to be done by the women. They were allowed to help out in gathering wood, preparing food, doing the various activities in food gathering, and fishing and hunting activities. During instructions or storytelling, the children were observed by the women. The children who listened and paid attention to the stories were the ones who will be the intellects, the thinkers, the philosophers, and the teachers. The children who fidgeted or did not pay proper attention are the ones who will be the hunters, fishermen, providers, and warriors.

All of this was taught in the language so that the children could hear the speakers and see their actions. This was done for the children that were up to seven years old. The children that were eight to thirteen years old still liked to listen to the at-soh-kaan-nun (the traditional stories) and they would soon start to tell their own. Those young children were now out on the land with their fathers, uncles, grandfathers, and older brothers. At this stage of learning the men were now involved. The older children were now participating in hunting and gathering expeditions and fishing activities. This next level of learning is more hands-on and practical. The children begin to watch both males and females go about completing their activities in the hunting and gathering society. They begin to do the activities themselves. Always present was the language that was used in everyday activities, the songs and prayers used to give thanks to the Creator and to the spirits of the animals, plants, fish, and water for giving them sustenance.

In the Anishinaabay language there is no word for "I am sorry." We didn't use it because it is considered an excuse for not doing something that you should know how to do. There was the notion that you were taught everything so adults were not to make mistakes that would endanger their family or other members of the nation. Children made mistakes, but they were supposed to learn from it. Usually mistakes were laughed at and people teased you about them. Humour was used to correct negative behaviour. Children were hardly scolded or disciplined by their parents. If a child was making trouble due to their behaviour it was the aunt or uncle that stepped in to correct the behaviour by telling the child directly or through a story. A parent's silence towards their child or just one glare can also tell the child to smarten up and change their ways.

The children are now experienced on how to behave on the land, lakes, and rivers during the four seasons. They watch and participate in all the activities during the different seasons. They are able to gather firewood, fetch water, pick berries, and watch the everyday activities of daily living. They are able to hunt small game like rabbit and partridge. It was considered a big event whenever someone made a first kill of an animal for the family to eat. The animal was prepared and cooked. There was a ceremony performed to offer prayer and thanks for the life of the animal. The child now knows that he or she is a provider.

By this time the oral language has expanded the children's vocabulary. The words, phrases, sentences, and the descriptions used on the land and in the wigwam are now varied. The children hear how the women use the language. They also hear how the young men, the male adults, and elders use the language. The children at this stage still enjoy storytelling. The children are also getting ready to enter into the next stage of their education. The next stage is one of the greatest changes that will happen during their life. The next stage is for children who are fourteen to nineteen years old. This is called the fast life. Though they are not kids anymore, they are yet to be adults.

Life changes for them now. The pace of life now increases with more responsibilities, more ceremonial teachings, and more participation in adult life. When girls start their menstrual cycle, they are now considered women. They begin the strawberry ceremony. This will last for a whole year. The boys at this stage will have their voice change and this will be the start of their vision quest. This also will last for a year.

The young girls are taught by their mothers with the help of women elders. This is the female academy. This is the beginning of using the formal language used by females. The girls are placed in special huts by themselves in the woods during their menstrual cycle. They are allowed to bring their arts and crafts and their sewing, and they sing and pray during this time. During their menstrual cycle the women have great power and their dreams and visions are very important. This is when they have time to reflect about their dreams and their meanings. They are brought out after a few days. The mothers and women elders ask the girls what their dreams and visions were and they figure out the meaning of the dreams. The mother, the sponsors, and the elders talk about the future of the girl and what her purpose in life is going to be. She could be a healer, a leader, a teacher, or a great warrior.

The boys are taught the men's teachings. This is the men's academy. The men use a formal language used in certain ceremonies and in other settings like tribal Councils. The ceremonies are delivered in the language as prayers, chants, and songs. The boys go into the wilderness with no food or water for several days. They can stay in a small wigwam or stay outside. A dream or vision will come to the boys and they are told to remember everything they saw and heard. They are brought back to the village to talk about their experiences with their father and the male elders. The boys are told the meaning of their dreams and visions. They are told what their responsibilities will be and what their purpose in life is going to be. The boys are then trained to become teachers, providers, healers, guardians, leaders, and warriors.

The boys and girls already have their Anishinaabay names from the naming ceremony. They have the four sponsors that were assigned to them. Their names will guide them to their purpose and the sponsors, elders, and their parents will help them. This will take a full year to complete. At the end of the ceremony in guiding the young people, there is a final feast to recognize them as men and women. From this time on the boys and girls start using the formal language used in all ceremonies and in talking to their elders and to the other adults.

The boys and girls are very busy at this stage of learning. Their newfound status in the community is recognized by everyone in the village. They have to watch what they say, and their behaviour has to be respectful. They will receive more training to look after themselves and others in the wilderness. It is not merely about survival, but it is also about living with nature.

The Anishinaabay education system prepared everyone to have a strong spirit before they enter into the next world. We want to say we did everything to live up to our names. Our language gives us our thoughts and ideas. We dream in the Anishinaabay language when we use the language fluently. Our inner thoughts are in the Anishinaabay language. They come from the spirit world. We talk to our Mah-nih-toog (Spirits) in our Anishinaabay languages.

This is a brief outline of the Anishinaabay education system before European contact. During the following years and even to this present day, our education system is outlawed by the federal and provincial governments. Native studies and native language programs are now taught in schools, but they are not funded properly and are not administered by us. We have lost the legal and administrative process to deliver our Anishinaabay education system the way it operated before European contact. We are told by the state that we don't know how to run our programs in our own communities the way it needs to operate. What Anishinaabay community right now has 100 per cent fluent Anishinaabay language usage?

Tah-wish-pih-mih-cih-won (It is still flowing).
The spirit of all living things is found on the land.

CHAPTER 4

Nih-taa-wih-gih-win noo-pih-meeng
(Born in the bush)

I am only one story. There are more out there.

The loons landed, maang-goog kee pohn-nee-wug, in Washi Lake in the fall. They soon started their cries as I started mine. I was born. They wanted to know if I made the journey from the spirit world to where I was supposed to be. As they heard my cry, they migrated down south. It was late for them to still be in the north as all the other ducks and birds had already left. Our parents told us that when an Anishinaabay baby is born, there is an animal or bird that appears on that day. They are to be our guardian or our spirit protector. They show themselves to make sure we made it here safely. This is part of the Anishinaabay education system. All of us Anishinaabayg are connected through this knowledge. The loons are my spirit birds. They are my protectors.

Washi Lake is located on the Albany River, which we call Kih-chi Zii-bii, meaning "big river." The river's head water is located in the Sioux Lookout area and it flows down into James Bay. Washi Lake is our ancestral, traditional land. No one else is allowed to hunt and fish in this area. The hunting and gathering society gives us the right to this area as it is laid out in our Anishinaabay languages. Our languages hold these laws and rights for us. This is where I was born, along with my two brothers, three sisters, and our cousins. All my relations were born on the land. This was our home, our classroom, our playground, and the passage for spiritual connection.

We did not speak a word of English. We only heard the Ojibway language. We only spoke the Ojibway language and we only dreamed in Ojibway. We are the last speakers from the fluent speakers. When our parents passed away, people said that the kings and queens left with only the jokers still here. We are the last generation of the old Ojibway language.

To this day in northern Ontario there are still Anishinaabay communities living with the language. They are considered isolated communities because there are no roads that lead to their villages. We Anishinaabayg do not consider ourselves as "isolated." There is no word in our Anishinaabay language to describe isolation. Growing up in the bush we felt no isolation at all. We grew up under the protection of our parents, grandparents, aunts, and uncles. The adults were always present. They were the masters that kept everyone safe and protected from harm. They all knew how to live off the land by being part of it. The animals, plants, water, and trees were all treated with respect. We were taught that we were not the masters of nature, but that we had to master the knowledge and secrets of the land around us.

Keshechiwon and Fort Albany are Cree communities situated where the mouth of the Albany River drains out into James Bay. The Hudson's Bay Company built a trading post there. They later moved inland to make more trading posts during the fur trade period. Going up the river from Keshechiwon and Fort Albany, the next community is Ogoki Post. This is where one of the most northerly Ojibway villages settled. Further up the river from Ogoki Post is where we have our ancestral land, the place where we were born. Even further up the river from Washi Lake is Makokibatan Lake, where our two uncles have their ancestral

land. From this lake, heading up the river, is the other most northern Ojibway nation, called Eabametoong. Eabametoong means
"reversing of the water place."

The Ojibway migrated from the east coast of Turtle Island long
before the Europeans arrived. Ways-kuch means "a long time ago."
This is how we measure time. We do not measure time in years.
Time is experience. It is not a number.

Ways-kuch we had seven mah-nih-toog (spirits) come to one
of our traditional ceremonies. There, they told the people about
the oncoming arrival of Europeans and encouraged us to move
out west. They said that the Anishinaabay Nation would be wiped
out in great numbers. We were told to move to the place where
food grows on the water. Villages that moved west were told that
when a white seashell appeared, we should continue moving.
White seashells will not be seen when we reached the destination.
The Anishinaabayg moved inland until they came upon food that
grew on the water. This was when they reached Kih-chi Ga-mee,
which is now called Lake Superior. In Kih-chi Ga-mee and in the
surrounding areas, they found wild rice growing in shallow bodies
of water. Our ancestors started settling around these lakes and
rivers. Anishinaabay communities started forming and the hunting and gathering societies maintained their lifestyle. But us Ojibway, we don't follow orders. Some of the village members started
exploring even further north and west. This is the reason why we
have Ojibway villages living at the foothills of the Rockies. It is
also why there are two Ojibway communities far to the north.

The words currently naming the Ojibway, Potawatomi, and
Odawa are pronounced using the colonial sounds that lose meaning through translation. Ojibway should be pronounced as "O-
zhi-bee-i-gay," meaning "he/she writes." Unlike other Indigenous
people, we wrote down our history on birch bark scrolls. Other

Anishinaabay villages called us O-zhi-bee-i-gay-i-ni-ni-wug, or "the People that Wrote." These scrolls are held by our scholars.

When the European explorers came and started settling on Turtle Island, we were already inland. The explorers planted two things on the land that changed our lives. The flag and the cross were the objects that gave the new arrivals permission to take over the new land. The first wave of settlers barely survived because they did not know how to live with the land. The eastern coastline of Turtle Island was populated by many different nations. The population of Europeans grew. The English, French, Spaniards, Portuguese, Dutch, and other nationalities, along with their native guides, travelled inland. The guides would be asked what village they were going to encounter next and they were told that it would be the O-zhi-bee-i-gay-i-ni-ni-wug. What the Europeans wrote down was what they heard phonetically, and that is why we ended up with the name "Ojibway."

The meaning that is in the history books says that Ojibway means "puckered." They say this is because we made our moccasins with the seams facing outwards, or that we cooked our meat over the fire until it became puckered. The only time I saw an Ojibway that had anything to do with "puckered" was when they puckered their lips for a kiss, or they were pointing with their lips. There are over twenty different ways of spelling O-zhi-bee-i-gay-i-ni-ni-wug; Ojibway, Ojibwe, Ojibwa, Chippewas, Chippewa, Otchipe, and other ways similar to these spellings.

The Potawatomi are another nation that has their original names said and written differently. They are called Poh-tah-way-i-ni-ni-wug, meaning "the People of the Fire." Poh-tah-way is a word that means "he or she is making a fire." The Potawatomi are the Fire Keepers of the Anishinaabay Nation. Their responsibilities are to keep the ceremonial fires of the Anishinaabayg alive. They keep our prayers, songs, and ceremonies strong, and they often perform them in our communities.

The Odawa Nation of the Anishinaabayg is also written and pronounced incorrectly. We call them A-taa-way-i-ni-ni-wug, meaning "the People of Commerce." This nation looked after the trading system of the Anishinaabayg. They knew all the trade routes of Turtle Island. The A-taa-way-i-ni-ni-wug bought, traded, and sold goods with the various villages.

The O-zhi-bee-i-gay-i-ni-ni-wug, the Poh-tah-way-i-ni-ni-wug, and the A-taa-way-i-ni-ni-wug formed the Three Fires Confederacy. This association protected each other whenever one of them was threatened with war from other villages or nations. We were a force to be reckoned with, but only when we were attacked. Basically, we were just basket weavers peacefully working on our art.

We are now in one of the greatest battles within ourselves. We have some fluent speakers left in the Three Fires Confederacy. But our fires are slowly dying out. The battle we now have is to keep our identity. To keep it, we need to have every Anishinaabay community talk in our language. Our language will need to be operating at the same level as it was operating at before European contact. We are not Canadian. We are Anishinaabayg.

May-in-gun (Wolf).
The flowing water has been here before European contact.
It is still flowing now and it will continue into the future.

PART TWO

Ish-poh too-kin-nih-goh-yung
(Before contact)

Omaa Miskohtesih Minising kiipahtenihwug Anishinaabayg
ispoh tahgohsihnaanihwung.
(Here on Turtle Island, there were a lot of Anishinaabayg
before contact.)
Kakina awenen ogiinisihtohtaan Anishinaabemowin.
(Everyone understood the Anishinaabay language.)
Kakina awenen giikahkitowug Anishinaabemowin.
(Everyone talked the Anishinaabay language.)
Kakina awenen giiemihcihgewug Anishinaabemowin.
(Everyone prayed in the Anishinaabay language.)
Kakina awenen gii inendumohwug Anishinaabemowin.
(Everyone thought in the Anishinaabay language.)
Kakina awenen giipahwaamohwug Anishinaabemowin.
(Everyone dreamed in the Anishinaabay language.)
Anishinaabeg ogiiahyaanahwaa Pahgitinigaywinun.
(Anishinaabayg had laws.)
Tawish noongohm atewon Anishinaabay Pahgitinigaywinun.
(Still today, they are still here, the Anishinaabay Laws.)
Niswi Pahgitinigaywinun: 1. Kihcih Manito Pahgitinigaywinun;
   2. Aki Pahgitinigaywinun; 3. Inini Pahgitinigaywinun

(Three Laws: 1. Great Spirit Laws; 2. Laws of the Land; 3. Laws
   of the People)
Anishinaabay Kahkihnohmaagewinun giiahte omaa Anishi-
   naabay akiing.
(Anishinaabay Teachings were here on Anishinaabay land.)
Kahnihtahwihgihnaanihwung kakina awenen ohgiinoon-
   daanaawaa atsohgahnun.
(When everyone is born, everyone heard the traditional stories.)
Atsohgahnun kiiahbahcihcihkaatewon cihkihkencihgahteg
   Anishinaabay bihmaatihziwin.
(The traditional stories were used so that it will be known,
   the Anishinaabay life.)
Abihnoochiinsug ogiiminwendahnahwah cihnoondahmo-
   hwaach atsohgahnun.
(The children were happy to hear the traditional stories.)
Nanabush, Wiisahkejaak anduhm Anishinaabayg okii-
   izhikaanahwaa ohwetih aabihtah manito aabihtah inini.
(Nanabush, Wiisahkejaak some Anishinaabayg they named
   this half-spirit, half-man.)
Tahtihbaacihmohwinun Nanabush wiinge ohminwendaan
   cih Anishinaabay.
(The stories say Nanabush really liked being an Anishinaabay.)
Nanabush ogiinahgahcihyaan Ogokomun omaa Anishinaabay
   akiing.
(Nanabush looked after his grandmother here on the Anishinaabay land.)
Wiinje giimandahwihzih; giibimose omaa akiing cih wiin-
   dahmahgech awihyaashiisug cih izhinihkaazohwaach; wiinje
   giinihtaa-andahwencihge; wiinge giinihtum; giinihtahmiigih-
   ndihzih awihyaaziizhug; giinihtaapahpihyaagunihwih; giiah-
   nihmihzih; wiingekiiminwendahgohzih.

(He really was a magician; he walked here on the land to tell
   what the animals were to be named; he really was a good
   hunter; he was really lazy; he really liked teasing the animals;
   he was always laughed at; he always acted like a baby; he was
   really liked.)

Wiinge mahwach Anishinaabayg ogiimissawendaanahwaa
   cih minotahtihbahcihmohwaach owenihwon tahtihbahcih-
   mohwinun.

(It was a great desire for Anishinaabayg to be really good storytellers with these stories.)

Anduhm eta Anishinaabayg gii-inohsihwug cih kih-cih kahkit-
   tohwininini.

(Only some Anishinaabayg were chosen to be orators.)

Abihnoochiinsug, oshkihniigihwug okiikihkendaanahwah
   Anishinaabemowin ebihzihndahmohwaach kicihahyaag
   aniinmahyaam wewenih cih kakitohwaach.

(Children, young people knew how to speak the Anishinaabay
   language by listening to the parents and elders on how to
   properly use the language when speaking.)

Ahmiiwetush Anishinaabemowin eoncihgiiancihseg.

(That is how the Anishinaabay language was transferred.)

Ahmiiwetush Anishinaabay Kihkendaasohwin.

(That is the Anishinaabay Knowledge.)

CHAPTER 5

An-dah-way-jih-gay-win pih-maa-tis-sih-win
(Hunting and gathering society)

Quee-queesh is the word for grey jay in the Ojibway language. The word for baby Quee-queesh is "Quee-queeshshayns." The "ayns" is the suffix to show the diminutive form. My Mom and Dad gave me the Ojibway name Quee-queeshayns. The baby birds have black faces when they are born and eventually will have white patches when they become adults. As I was growing up, I played outside most of the time and I would come back inside with a black face from all the dirt or mud. I was a baby bird.

I grew up along the banks of the Albany River. I was born on Washi Lake in northern Ontario, about halfway between Sioux Lookout and James Bay.

On the day I was born three loons landed on Washi Lake. The calendar date was 23 October 1954. It was late for them to be up north as all the other ducks and birds had already migrated south. There was ice along the shoreline. The Anishinaabayg, the People, believe that this means the loons are my spirit birds. They brought me in from the spirit world and they were there to make sure that I arrived safely in the physical world. These birds are my guardians. They heard me cry and then they left. They are my connection to the water, land, and air.

Throughout my life there are always loons around me. They are on the lakes and rivers that I am on. Once I was on an island with a back bay. It was early in the morning and there were four loons swimming on the calm water. I happen to look at them and they formed a circle with one to the east, one to the south, one to the west, and one to the north. They sat on the water covering the four cardinal points and seemed to say, "Watch this, Baxter." They started swimming in a circle going from east to west. When they came back to their original places, they stopped swimming and looked inward to the circle. The loon from the east rose from the water, just skimming over the top, and when it reached the western loon, they all dove into the water. I thought that was fascinating.

A few years later I told this to an elder and she told me that I needed to feed the loons. How am I to do that? I could not stand by a lake and feed the loons. But the elders do this all the time. They tell you what to do but do not give you specifics. This is a learning strategy where it is up to you to find the answer. I thought about it for a couple more years and then asked another elder. They told me that I needed to go into the sweat lodge to do a ceremony for the loons. This is a spiritual feeding. I have not gone in yet, so for now I talk to the loons in Ojibway whenever we meet on the lake.

If you hear me talking to the loons one day, don't think I'm a lunatic.

I wasn't taught these traditional teachings because I went to residential school. They took these teachings away from me. My gift is the knowledge I have in the Anishinaabay language. I still use the language whenever I am with other fluent speakers. I have taught the language in Anishinaabay communities. It has been a while since I had a dream in the language.

I was teaching in Whitedog, now called Wabihsihmong, in the early 1980s. This is an Anishinaabay community just north of Kenora, Ontario. It was my first year teaching and I was assigned to teach grade eight. One day we took the grade seven and eight students for a cultural workshop to Kenora. We stayed overnight at the Friendship Centre and in the morning I was talking to some of the elders giving cultural teachings. These were respected elders from the surrounding area. I started talking about my experience and told them about residential school. I said that, because of residential school, I did not know what my Clan was. I knew the loon was my spiritual bird, but I heard that my father might belong to the Caribou Clan, which in Ojibway is the Attick Clan. I then said that if I put them together, I would then belong to the "loon-attick" clan.

I thought that was funny, but they didn't. I was never invited to their cultural teachings again.

As a baby I was a problem child. I refused to drink my Mom's breast milk. My parents could not figure out what was wrong, so they asked my grandfather what to do. He said he had a dream about it and said that he will never accept his mother's milk. We were living up the river from the reserve on our traditional lands. The Hudson's Bay Company had a store far away. My Dad and grandfather walked to the store to get cases of Carnation milk. They walked all day and night. They came back with enough milk for me to last until the spring. I still love the taste of Carnation milk.

The first year of my life I was wrapped in a waapihcheepihsohn, a soft moose hide cloth casing that had strings on both sides to be pulled tight over the baby. My Dad made all the cradle boards for us children and he was asked by other parents to make one for their children. He was a great artisan.

After spending the first year wrapped up like an Indian corn-dog, I was ready to walk on the land. My Mom and Dad raised six of us on the land. Two of my brothers died on the land. I do not remember them. One of them drank some water from a beaver pond and died from it. The other one caught a bad cold with a fever and passed away.

Growing up, I wasn't fully aware that my three older sisters were going to residential school at this time. They would be home for July and August but went back to the school from September until the end of June. My younger brother, Jerry, and my older brother, Angus, who was only a year and a half older than me, all stayed with our parents out on the land. I was also not aware when my older brother went to residential school.

During that autumn there would only be my younger brother Jerry, our Mom and Dad, and myself living together. Eventually it would only be our Mom and Dad left on the land. It was years later, as an adult, I thought about my Mom and the total silence she endured when all of us were taken to residential school. I cried for her. Her ancestral knowledge and her language transfer to us diminished.

My Mom told me years later that Dad had decided to keep me with them so that one of us boys would learn the ways of living the ancestral life. My Dad was a provider, a teacher, a protector, a guide, and a great storyteller. I disappointed him by demanding to go to school.

Washi Lake is on the Albany River and it is up the river from the Ogoki Post reserve. We belong to the Marten Falls Band. I was born on this lake. It is our ancestral land. This was where we grew up in our formative years. Our Mom and Dad, our uncle John and his family, and our grandparents all lived on the lake. There was a tourist camp on the sandy point. Our father and uncle guided the

American fishermen and moose hunters through the bush during
the summer and fall seasons. We lived in the log houses that our
Dad and uncle built for us. This was our base camp. We lived the
nomadic lifestyle. There were other camp sites we went to during
the four seasons. We rotated camp sites so that the animals there
could replenish.

Another person living on the lake during summer was a prospector. He had a camp further down the lake from us. We visited him
occasionally. Our Dad, uncle, and grandfather took him around
the area to do surveys. Once, a float plane landed on our dock
looking for the prospector. It happened on a day that my brothers,
sisters, and cousins went for a walk along the shore without me.
A plane landing was always a big event for us. I must have been
about five years old at the time. Our Mom never came down to
the plane. So, it was just my aunt and I to meet the plane. Both of
us didn't know a word of English. The pilot wanted to know where
the prospector was. My aunt started pointing with her lips to the
place where they took the prospector. The pilot left.

That evening our Dad came back. I went into the cabin.

He asked, "Kih-gee-shig nah?" ("Did you pee?)"

I said, "Ayah." "(Yes.)"

He said, "Kih-zeen-geen!" ("Wash your hands!)"

I said, "Kaa-ween nin-gee-toh-kih-naa-zee!" ("I didn't touch
him!)"

That cracked him up. I told my Mom and Dad that I wanted to
go to school. I said that when a Shaa-gun-aash, an English person,
was talking to me in their language I wanted to talk back to them
in their language, not just point with my lips. He cracked up on
that, too.

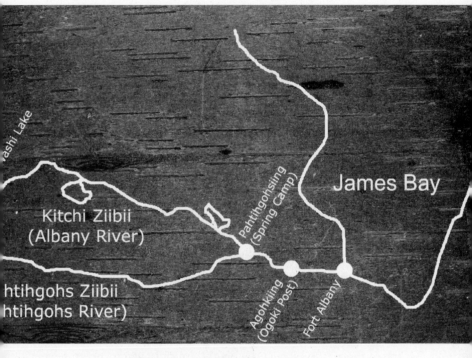

Map of the Kih-chi Zii-bii (Albany River).

CHAPTER 6

Kih-chi Zii-bii
(Albany River)

We grew up on Washi Lake only knowing the Anishinaabay language. We were taught in the language, gaining knowledge from our parents, aunt, and uncle, along with our grandparents. The social order, the early childhood education system, and our mental, physical, social, and spiritual development were given to us in the Anishinaabay education system in our language.

Our Anishinaabay language gives us the social order for us to survive on the land. We have certain protocols that we follow. One of them is to respect the plants, animals, water, air, and every living and non-living thing on the planet. Whenever we take the life of an animal for us to live, we say a prayer to the spirit of that animal. When the animal is killed there is a thank you prayer for giving its life so that we can live. There is also an offering of tobacco at the place where the animal was killed. This is a sacred ceremony in our Anishinaabay language that is still being done by traditional Anishinaabayg.

There is a sacred law that states we can't disrespect any parts of the animal by throwing it away. In this way we use every part of the animal. For example, when we killed a moose, we would use its meat for food; its hide was used for making sinew, which was also tanned using the moose brain to make clothes; its bones were used as scrapers and also were boiled to cook the marrow. The remaining animal parts were not given to our dogs.

The homes of the animals were not to be disturbed. Once, our Mom told us a story about our uncle Eli, who was a great hunter. One of his nicknames was An-joh, meaning "someone who had great abilities in hunting." He was out in the bush trapping beavers and he peed on a beaver house. After this, he couldn't trap a beaver, or any other animal for that matter. They would not allow themselves to be caught. He then struggled to provide for his family. Our uncle Eli went to see his Dad, our grandfather, about this trouble. Our grandfather questioned him about anything that he had done to disrespect the animals. Our uncle Eli told him about the beaver incident. Our grandfather told him to do a prayer and a ceremony to undo the disrespectful act. He did and was able to hunt again with much success.

We were a part of the hunting and gathering society that existed before European contact. Hunting, fishing, gathering, and spiritual activities were a part of our early learning education. The lakes, rivers, forest, and the sky were all part of our classroom. As children growing up along the Kih-chi Zii-bii (Albany River), we played, explored, observed, listened, hunted, fished, and gathered the knowledge of our ancestors. We learned all this in the Ojibway language. Our parents, aunts, uncles, and grandparents all spoke the Ojibway language. The language holds our Anishinaabay stories, our history, our curriculum, our science, our protocols, our laws, and our sacred ceremonies.

Once, my family and I were travelling in a sixteen-foot square-stern canvas canoe on one of the many tributaries of the Albany River. Our Mom was sitting at the front of the canoe and my younger brother Jerry and I were sitting in the middle of the canoe on one our packsacks. We were surrounded with blankets, clothes, food boxes, and other essential items all bundled in packs. This was in the springtime. We had the axe, buck saw, woodstove, our food utensils, pails, dishes, candles, gasoline, tent, radio, various traps, .30-30 rifle, shotgun, .22 rifle, ammunition, slingshots, files, and Mom's sewing kit; and attached at the back of the stern was a six-horse Johnson motor. Our Dad guides the motor through the many currents of the river. Looking at the shore we would spot one of our four dogs stopping to look at us and then continuing to run alongside us to keep up.

We did a portage with our Mom while our Dad shot the rapids with all of our stuff in the canoe. It was late spring at that time. The days were getting longer, and it was getting warmer. The trees didn't have leaves yet. We were placed in the middle of the canoe. Dad went to the back and Mom sat in the front. She pointed to a baby spruce tree growing out of a moss-covered log sticking out into the water. I remember her smiling at that.

Another time, my younger brother and I, along with our parents, travelled up the river from Washi Lake. Our brother and sisters were not home from residential school yet. It was late spring. We left early in the morning from the log cabin. We shot the first rapids with all of our gear in the canoe. There were a number of rapids and falls that we had to portage before we reached our uncle David and uncle Eli's hunting grounds. It was on a big lake called Ma-koh-koh-ba-tan Lake (Bear Lake). Uncle Eli had a cabin on an island along the north shore. Uncle David's cabin was just behind the island on the north shore and had a sandy point on it. At the other end of the beach there was a small river that came out of the wilderness. We moved further up along the north shore, where our parents were going to commercial fish with our uncle David and his family. We were the first to arrive.

Us kids would jump out of the canoe and start to collect stones for our slingshots. Our pockets were full of stones as we went up to the old camp site. Our uncle's camp is just a little to the west

side of our site. The tent frames stood there waiting for us to arrive. We walked past with our slingshots. Mom and Dad took everything out of the canoe. They put up the canvas tent. They
collected the spruce boughs for the flooring and placed them on
the ground. The stove was set up inside the tent. They put everything else inside. We wandered into the bush with our pockets full
of stones and our slingshots to bring down any squirrels, partridge, birds, or anything that moved, really. We never got anything. We shot up stumps, trees, branches, and fallen logs. We soon
ran out of stones. We stayed away from camp in case we might
have to do something for our parents. Then we found a pile of
moose poop.

The moose droppings were round, dried, and hard. We picked
them up and shot up stumps and trees with our slingshots. They
exploded into a dry dust cloud when we made a direct hit. I don't
how it started, but we soon had a moose poop war. Jerry had his
pile of moose poop and I had mine. We hid behind some trees in
the bush. When he hid his head behind one tree, I let one go. The
moose poop arrived at the side of the tree at the same time his
face reappeared. I got him square on the forehead. A cloud of
brown dust exploded over his face and went into his eye. There
was a moment of silence and then his crying pierced the forest.
Our Dad came running over. I ran away.

We never did that again.

CHAPTER 7

Nin-gee-pah-maa-zha-gay-min
(We walk along the shore)

Commercial fishing was done in the summer. Our Dad and uncles made log cabins without windows. They had doors. During the winter months, they cut large blocks of ice from the frozen lake. Before the chainsaws they used long saw blades. The ice blocks were then pulled out using long ice tongs. They were dragged onto the ice and loaded on the toboggan. After they were secured to the toboggan with ropes, the dogs pulled them off the lake and up to the icehouse. The inside of the icehouse was full of sawdust. The ice blocks were piled up to the rafters and covered with the sawdust. Sawdust insulated the ice and prevented it from melting. The ice lasted throughout the summer. The doorway is blocked off with a slab of board.

Gill nets are used to catch the fish. Our parents made the gill nets using twine they bought from the Hudson's Bay Company store. It was long and it would be tangled up before it was set in the water. I was the one that helped with untangling the net. It was boring. A smooth wooden stick is placed between two tripods and it is about five to six feet above the ground. A pile of net is placed on the ground; I am on one side while Mom and Dad sit on the other side with a galvanized tub between them. One end of the net is placed over the wood and it is pulled down by Mom and Dad. I held onto the dirty net while they inspected and cleaned it. One takes the side with the floating bulbs and lays it carefully on one side of the tub. The other takes the side of the net that the leaded sinkers were on. I sat there wondering what my brothers and sisters were doing without me. My younger brother was too young to be doing this. My older brother was too old to be doing this. I was just right. Everyone else was out playing while I sat holding onto the net. It happened that there were a bunch of nets to be set.

Mom and Dad took me to set the nets. I steered the canoe with a paddle to keep it straight. I always wondered where everyone else disappeared to when it was time to set the nets. We went to designated areas to drop the nets. A rock is tied to the net to hold it in place. The first rock is placed over the side along with the first section of the net. It goes down until it hits the bottom of the lake. The leaded sinkers are placed first in the water and they sink the net. The buoyant floats stay on top of the water and keep the top part of the net up while the rest of the net is under the water. I paddle straight until the whole net is set in the water. At the end we paddle together to straighten it out even more while my parents still hold the end part. There is a rock used as an anchor that is attached to the bottom part of the net near the last sinker, and that is put in the water. As the net sinks, a long rope is let out until the net settles under the water. At the end of this rope there is a large floating marker that helps us locate the net when it is time to retrieve it.

We checked the nets every couple of days. The fish caught were entangled by the side of the canoe by Mom and Dad, with me steering the canoe to stay close to the net. The net is pulled up using the rope that is attached to the plastic marker. They started with the first buoyant float and lifted the net while standing. They took off the fish that were caught in the net by their gills. Some are still alive, but they get taken off and placed inside the galvanized tub. When a fish is caught, Mom and Dad kneel down and pull that portion of the net inside the canoe to untangle the fish. The fish would tangle the net so bad that it took some time to get it off. It also took time to straighten the net out again before Mom and Dad stood up to lift the net and check to see if it was good to continue. They pulled off any underwater grass, pieces of wood, or dead crayfish that were in the net. They did this until we reached the end of the net and all the fish were taken off. The thing that I never understood was that, as the net was being lifted up, they shook the water off the net. Why shake it off when it would be in the water again?

The fish we caught were pickerel (o-gans), whitefish (at-tick-kamayg), trout (manza-may-gos), pike (kih-noh-shay), catfish (man-zih), suckers (na-may-bin-nug), and sturgeon (na-may). The sturgeons grew so big, some over a hundred pounds. They are bottom feeders. Their mouths act as suction cups that vacuum the bottom of the lakes and rivers. They suck up crayfish, bloodsuckers, and insects that live under the rocks in the water. They used to jump out of the water as we travelled by in the canoe. They would roll over onto their backs in the air and create a big splash. They have pure white bellies and very hard, sharp, pointed armour covering both sides of their black bodies and also sharp ridges all along their back. The top of their heads is hard, and they have a long snout. These fish were here when the dinosaurs roamed the earth.

It was always hard to get a huge sturgeon into the canoe when it is still alive. The sturgeon was not killed right away. They are staked along the shore to keep them alive. A long rope is used to tie them to a strong stick driven down into the earth. The other end of the rope is pushed through the gills and out of their mouths. They are not able to bite through the rope as they don't have any teeth. The sticks were a few feet apart along our side of the shore.

Because the other fish were smaller, they were cleaned right away. The guts are taken out and the fish are washed. They are put in the tub and driven to the icehouse to be frozen until the service float plane arrived. A fish buyer came by about once every two weeks to collect the fish. The fish are weighed and sold to the buyer. He came by our camp with a small Cessna 180 with floats on its legs. He also brought food supplies that were ordered from the previous trip.

The sturgeon are pulled up from their tether, gutted, cleaned, and weighed when the plane lands in the lake. This ensures that they are sold fresh. Sturgeon also had their roe taken out, weighed, and sold. They are used to make caviar, which is very expensive.

While waiting for the fish buyer to arrive I would walk along the shoreline whistling to make sure no one else was around. I approached the stick along the shore that the biggest sturgeon was tied to. I slowly and silently pulled the rope towards me. A black log appears from the deep gently coming to me. At my feet I would turn the sturgeon back towards the deep part of the lake. It lay silently at the bottom of the shallow part of the lake close to the shore. I grabbed its tail. It made a splash as it flicked its body and smoothly glided away from me towards the deep. It looked like a black torpedo. Before it vanished, I pulled on the rope tied to it and it turned over a couple of times. I saw the black and white of it as it tumbled under the water. I let the rope go after. I was just trying to have a little bit of fun.

Us kids played outside in the bush every day. My older brother, sisters, and cousins came home from residential school at the end of June. Nin-gee-pah-maa-zha-gay-min (we walked along the shore). There were a lot of activities to do as there were many of us. There were six children in our immediate family and we had eleven cousins. Our log cabins were on the north shoreline with plenty of stones and rocks to play with. Along the shore going to the east end of the lake there was Nay-aa-sheeng (a place with long tall reeds growing close to the shore). At this place we had the icehouse for the fish we caught and sold. To the west of us we walked along the shoreline where there were long tall reeds in the water and there was a small bay. This bay continued as a beach to a point about a half-mile long. This was where we swam most of the day. We called this Nay-taa-wung-gang meaning "the place where there is sand." The beach ended with a long sandy point that jutted out into the bigger part of Washi Lake. There was also a larger part of the lake west of the sandy point, and even further out there was another lake we called A-wus-sih-gam, meaning "the lake on the other side."

Directly south of the sandy point there was a short, stony beach. We hardly went there. Up the river from there, on the south shore, the Albany River entered into Washi Lake. There was a small rapid that we went up, and there were other falls up the river before we were able to reach Ma-ko-ko-ba-tan Lake. This was a big lake where two uncles and their families lived. We hardly saw them. At the east end of Washi Lake, the river flowed out and continued until it reached the west side of James Bay.

One of our favourite activities was to wade into the shallow water with our pants rolled up and catch fish with our bare hands. We filled up pails of water and placed them along the shore. When we found a round, flat rock, we turned it over slowly and placed it gently beside its original location. Two types of fish hid under these rocks. One of them was a small fish with a big head. Its body tapered to the tail and it had large side fins. We called it pah-koh-kohn-nih-choo (a chubby fish). The other fish is the man-zih (baby catfish). It usually is long and black. The fish thought that the flat rock overhead was protecting them. We kept our hands flat and approached the fish from both sides of the rock. When the fish are between our hands, we cupped them close with the fish inside. The fish were taken to the pails on the shore and we dumped them in. After we did this for a while, we gathered around the pails to see who caught the biggest, the prettiest, and the smallest fish. The fish were then dumped back into the water. We did this again the following week.

We usually got a fright whenever we turned over a rock and an a-zhaa-gayns (a crayfish) would look up to us as it backed away with its claws in a defensive position. It would be saying, "Oh yeah, come on, I'll take you on!" To catch one of these we put our fingers in front of it and while it tried to fight off our frontal approach, we grabbed it from its tail with our other hand. We took it to the shore and showed our dogs to it. We put the crayfish on their nose, and they shook it off. It flew off the nose and landed back in the water.

Chee-way-gun-noo, the one that flies silently, is the dragonfly. They were always around us. We saw a variety of them. One of them we called Ki-chi Mo-ko-man-a-kee, which means "The Land of the Big Knives" while also referring to the United States. It had a green, slender body and it folded its wings when it was resting. It pushed off from its resting place and opened its wings with a massive motion. The wings looked like they were moving all over the place. Another one was the transport carrier, a large dragonfly with a blueish tinge to its body. Its wings jutted out from its body and it silently flew straight for a while until it suddenly turned to catch a flying bug. The bug is pulled close by the dragonfly using its legs and folding it into its body, holding it tight. It flies to a tree to stop and eat its prey. This one has large compound eyes. They flew by us and stopped in mid-air and changed its direction. It was challenging to shoot them with our slingshots.

Our younger sister, Wanda, was a tomboy who was far better than us boys in running, swimming, throwing, fishing, hunting, and in using the slingshot. We had three older sisters and Wanda was the youngest of them. We looked up to her. She had deadly aim with a slingshot. A dragonfly would be flying by and she would take the head off of it. The dragonfly would keep flying without its head. She was very good. Our other sisters were too old for this.

We caught the bigger chee-way-gun-noo alive. We took a dry branch to catch it as it was resting on a tree or when it flew too close to us. The dry branches held the dragonfly down. We picked it up on its back just behind its back wings. The long tail is tied with a thread and we let it go. The chee-way-gun-noo flies away while we hold onto the string. We ran after the dragonfly as it flew. This was fun for a while, but we always untied them and let them fly away.

Wanda, the tomboy, stole some matches from our Mom one day. It was bad for her to do this and we were going to tell on her. She said she would teach us how to smoke just like Mom. We said we won't tell on her then. She did not have Mom's cigarettes, but she said that's okay because she knew where to get some. We followed her along the shore away from our cabin. She started looking for something along the shoreline. Wanda picked up a dried reed stalk from the shore. The reed stalk was broken into the length of a cigarette. This is how to smoke, she said. The match was struck just like how Mom did it and Wanda lit the reed. We saw her inhale the stalk, and she suddenly spit it out from her lips, grabbing her throat. The dried cinders of the stalk inside had caught on fire and she inhaled them. She ran to the water and took in huge gulps of it. We laughed so hard. She never did that again.

One day I was playing outside by the log house. I happened to look underneath the house. I saw the logs on the ground that held up the rest of the house. Between two logs there was a waa-bih-goh-sheesh (mouse) sitting on the ground eating something. I quietly went inside to tell Wanda to get her sling shot. I told her about the mouse. We went outside and bent down on the ground to have a look. She whispered to me that she was going to go to the other side and I was to keep an eye on the mouse. I saw Wanda at the other side and the mouse was between us. The last thing I remembered was her pulling back on her sling shot. She came back to where I was and asked me if she got the mouse. She soon realized that I was staggering around with a blood spot in the middle of my forehead. I guess she hit the mouse and also me in the process. She wiped the blood off my forehead and told me not to tell our parents.

We also made our own fishhooks to catch fish. Our Dad helped by cutting open the top of empty Carnation milk cans. The top lids are cut into triangles. The top part of the triangle is wider, and two incisions are cut, one on each side. The top part is where we tied the thread, and that is tied to the fishing pole. The fishing pole we use is a dried stick. The hook is bent at the sharp point to catch the fish. A chunk of lard is used for bait. Fish love lard. We sat at the end of the wooden dock with our pails of water. A-chow-ayns-sag (small perch) swam around the dock along with minnows.

We caught the fish and they were placed into the pails full of water. After a while we stopped fishing and counted how many each of us caught. We always wanted to be the ones that caught the biggest fish. We did the judging and we dumped the fish back into the water until next time.

Our Dad made us boats to play with in the water. He split a dried piece of wood and fashioned the boats out of it. He shaped the wood into a canoe by cutting one end into a point. The other end he left alone to make a square stern. The middle part of the wood is carved out with a curved knife to make the interior of the canoe. A nail is placed at the pointed part of the wood and a piece of string is tied to it. The string is then tied to a stick. We run along the shore holding the stick out and the boat is dragged along on top of the water. We made the sound of a motor as we ran up and down the shoreline. We placed stones on the boat to represent our father, mother, and us kids.

My older brother Angus and I were playing with our boats one morning. We had travelled down the shoreline from our place to a little creek running into the lake. It was a good spot as it had small rapids to test our skills in running the rough waters. The source of the water was a huge swamp full of dark water. It had fast-moving currents and it was a challenge to get our boats up the currents without losing the passengers. It was a quiet morning until we heard a loud noise in the bush. We looked at each other, dropped our sticks, and ran. Screaming and crying, we ran home along the shore as fast as we could. My older brother took off his shoes to run faster but the hard stones hurt his feet. I ran past him and did not look back. Hearing our screams, our Dad came down to the shoreline with his tea in his hand.

"Bear! Bear!" we cried as we ran past him and up to the tent. Bears, especially mother bears with their cubs, could be dangerous.

He stayed behind at the shore for a while and finally came up to the tent. We were panting and trying to catch our breath when he entered the tent. He sat down and poured himself more tea and in a calm voice said that the bear we saw was just our dog, August, roaming around in the bush. He burst out laughing.

The dog came out of the bush and back to the tent. We went back to racing our boats in the rough water near the swamp.

CHAPTER 8

Zhoo-kih-pohn
(It begins to snow)

At the end of August, the float plane came to take our older brother and sisters away. It was time for them to return to residential school. We wouldn't see them again until the end of June the following year. This was a sad day. There was crying. I was oblivious to all this. I only wanted to play.

The plane is loaded down with our brother, sisters, and cousins. The plane left the dock with a blast of air as the engine was started. It slowly moved away from the shore and got smaller. The plane turned into the wind; the pilot put the wing flaps down and opened up the engine. The noise got louder and the back-spray of water behind the plane blew round. The plane plowed through the lake, the floats cutting the water in two parts, creating a hump of water between the two waves. The floats rose out of the water, dripping as the plane went higher into the air until it was just a dot in the sky. The noise of the plane diminished as it went closer to the small town where it was taking our brother, sisters, and cousins. We heard the plane no longer. It was quiet.

Sometimes our Dad wouldn't be there to see them leave as he would be up or down the river guiding American fishermen. I picture him in the middle of the rapids, holding a kaan-da-kee-win-naak (wooden pole) in the water to keep the canoe steady for the

Americans to catch fish. He hears the plane land and then leave with his children that he won't see until next June. The Americans continue to laugh and carry on while trying to catch fish.

Mom takes us back to the cabin to wait for our Dad to return. It seemed that everything stopped. There wasn't anyone left for me to go fishing with, no one to run our boats with, and no one to walk with along the shore. We were with silence. Pretty soon the birds and ducks will also be going south. Everything would be still. I was still a child. I only wanted to play.

When they leave, it is only my younger brother, our mother, our father, our dogs, and I.

It gets colder. The leaves change colour. Ice starts to form close to the shoreline. The ice is not safe to walk on. It only freezes a short distance from the shoreline. Open water is still seen on the lake. There were still some stones not frozen, so we took our slingshots and shot these stones across the ice. The stones glided and skipped along the ice with a "kching, kching, kching" sound until they disappeared under the water. We threw bigger stones onto the ice that glided on the surface without breaking it. Somehow, they seemed to slow down before they plunged into the cold water forever.

The waa-bun-non-goh-zeeg (the snow buntings) arrived when the snow came on the land. The place where they came from is further north where it is colder. They are brown, black, and white. They fly in huge flocks. They land on the shoreline to eat. Our grandfather blasted them with his double-barrel shotgun. He picked up the birds he had killed; he cleaned them and had a great meal.

Grandfather was a great hunter. Our Mom told us about the time he killed three ducks with a single shot. The ducks were pah-kah-kooh-shi-bug (the golden-eye). These ducks always seem to fly in groups of three. They seem to be going to a big meeting in the sky and they are late. The story goes that grandfather saw three of them approaching and he hid in the bushes. He stood up and aimed. The three ducks briefly stopped in mid-air to separate and go in different directions. At that brief hesitation in their flight he fired the one shot. All three of them came tumbling down from the sky!

One fall before our brother Angus went to residential school, we saw a huge flock of waa-bun-non-goh-zeeg fly by and land at the bend before the sandy beach. We gathered as many stones as we could and put them in our pockets. We walked slowly through the bush to sneak up on them, as they were skittish. We had to pass by our uncle's cabin and then our grandparent's cabin. We approached the point where we thought the birds had landed. They weren't there. We walked onto the shoreline and the huge flock of birds took off further up along the shore. Our grandfather came out of the bush close to where the birds took off. He had his double barrel shotgun. He walked right by us without saying a word. We got the silent treatment. We spoiled his hunt. He was mad!

Winter came. We call October "Bin-naa-quee Gee-sis," the month of shedding leaves. We saw the leaves change colour and fall down from the trees. The ones that landed on the water soon washed up on the shore. Some leaves sank into the ponds that develop on flat rocks that have a shallow curve to them. Then came Kash-kah-dun Gee-sis, the month where everything is frozen tight. You may better know this as November. The snow and ice covered everything, even our grandmother's axe.

Our grandparents lived in their own log cabin. It was always cozy. The cabin was to the west of ours. There was a little trail leading up to their house. We visited our grandmother when the men went out trapping. She always had hot bannock with raisins ready for us to eat. Bannock is a mixture of flour, baking soda, and melted lard. It is cooked over the stove in a big frying pan greased with lard. She added raisins to make it sweet. The bannock is broken open and steam comes out of it. We slathered it with lard. It was so good! She always hid her knives, scissors, and axe from us as we always wanted to help around the log cabin. We arrived for a visit once and Grandma was outside looking for something. She had misplaced her axe in the snow; she forgot where she buried it to keep it away from us. We helped her find it, but she still didn't let us use it.

My favourite activity in winter was sliding down our hill. Our toboggan was made by our Dad. He found a good size birch tree about eight feet high. It had no twist in its grain and no knots. He cut it down with his axe. He split the tree in half using dried wood wedges he made using the wood nearby. Dad chopped the tree halves with his axe into two rough boards. He brought them back to the outside drawing log he had made. It was a log placed on two stumps. The log was shaved down to a flat surface. It had a raised platform near the ends. This was where the wood to be shaved was placed. The raised platform stopped the wood that was being shaved from sliding off. Dad had a hand-held wood shaver that he used to make the rough boards into two slabs of thin wood for the toboggan. The wood shaver is a flat piece of steel that has an adjustable blade coming out of a slanted hole at the bottom. The top part of the shaver has a wooden handle at the back and a wooden knob near the front. Dad shaved the wood to the desired width. Long, curled, shaved wood came out after every stroke and fell to the ground. It made good kindling.

The two shaved boards have holes drilled into them by Dad using a hand-held drill that had a drill bit attached to it. The boards are slashed together with moose hide string. The front end of the toboggan is placed through two trees standing close together. The front part of the boards has a thick board nailed to it. Moose hide string is attached loosely on both sides for now. On the top part of the toboggan he drilled holes into the two railings that have been nailed along the edges of the boards. The top part of the toboggan is slowly bent between the two trees. This is done so that the front part of the toboggan has a permanent curve to it. The boards are held to the desired curved and the moose hide string is tied to the top railings to keep the curve in place.

The toboggan is put inside to dry out. The wooden railings on top of the boards have holes drilled into them and a piece of rope is laced through the holes. The rope is used to hold onto the toboggan when it was being pulled up a hill. There are several long ropes attached on both sides of the toboggan that are used to hold down the load that was being pulled. A large canvas covering is placed over the toboggan. When our belongings were put on the toboggan the canvas is pulled over to cover all the belongings. The strings are then weaved through the entire bundle by tying them on the string of the toboggan.

When the toboggan was not in use by our Dad, we went down the hill with all the ropes tucked into the sides. The curved front of the toboggan is held onto while we run along the side of it before jumping on. Both sides of the curved part are held onto as the toboggan went down the hill. My brother Angus always went further than me. I tried so hard to beat him. I couldn't do it.

It was two days before Christmas when a plane landed on the lake. The pontoon landing gear had been replaced by skis. The men went on the plane to sell furs at the Ogoki Post reserve nearby. There was a Hudson's Bay Company store there where everyone sold their fur. At this time the fur prices were high, but the money went to paying off the debts that were incurred by the trappers to buy supplies. They paid off their debts and put more into their credit to supply themselves for the rest of the winter. Our father, uncle, and grandfather came back later that day with presents and supplies. Dad gave me a new sleigh that Christmas. It had steel runners with handlebars at the front. Angus never beat me again at tobogganing. The wooden body was flat, and I was able to lie on it going down the hill. With enough speed I could speed down the hill and end up halfway across the lake.

Mom and Dad said that I would get up by six a.m. to go sledding in the winter. I went up and down the hill by myself all the time. They said that I would come back to our log cabin and stand by their bed, crying. They asked what was wrong. I told them that I had no one to go sliding with me. Everyone my age was at residential school. The sun wasn't even up yet.

We stayed at Washi Lake during the winter months as it was our base camp. Our grandparents and our uncle with his family made up the community. The men went out into the trap line to check their traps. They brought the animals back to be skinned. These were beaver, otter, marten, mink, rabbit, squirrel, and sometimes a lynx. Mom and Dad skinned the animals using a sharp curved knife. The hides are cleaned by scraping off the meat and fat. The beaver hides are put on a square stretcher made up of four sticks. The corners of the stretcher are braced with shorter sticks to hold the frames in place. The beaver hides are sewn into the frames using a big needle. The hide is placed inside the open frames, and the needle is pushed through the outside edges of the hide. The strong thread is tied in a knot at the end so that it won't come off. The thread then goes over the stick and is brought back to the edge of the beaver skin. The needle is pulled through the skin and pulled over the stick until the whole hide is stretched onto the frame. The framed beaver hides are hung up to dry inside the house. They are taken off when they dry and placed one on top of each other. They are put into a sack and put away until they are taken to the Hudson's Bay Company store to sell.

The otter, muskrat, squirrel, lynx, marten, and rabbit are also put on stretcher boards. These boards are carved until they are thin. They are made to have a point to them with square ends at the opposite end. The animals are skinned by their back legs first and the whole hide is pulled off. The hides are pulled inside out and they are placed on the stretcher. They are pulled down tight and the bottom ends of the hide are nailed to the board. They are also hung up to dry. After they become dry, the hides are taken off the boards and are turned around so that the fur is on the outside. Our Dad would come home for a couple of days before going out again to check his other traps.

We begged him, "At-soh-kayn! At-soh-kayn!" (Tell us stories! Tell us stories!).

Mom and Dad often told us stories about Weeshakayjaak. He was the main character in our oral stories. Weeshakayjaak was a trickster, a magician, half spirit and half man. He had special powers where he could turn himself into anything that he wanted to be. In their stories he wanted to be in the form of Anishinaabay, the original person. His grandmother was an Anishinaabay i-quay (Ojibway woman) and he always wanted to live with her. He was also a great hunter that could provide food for his grandmother. But he was lazy, at times stupid, and always forgot that he had special powers. He was funny and liked to tease the animals, but he also helped them when they needed it. There was always a misadventure for Weeshakayjaak. We knew that there was going to be something bad that would happen to him and these were teachings for us to learn and follow.

This is my favourite story about Weeshakayjaak called "Wee-sa-kay-jaak a-yaa-tush Misko-tay-sheens" (Weesakayjaak and the Turtle):

Wee-sa-kay-jaak pay-shi-koh keen-doh-kee-gohns-shi-kay.
A-sha ween-gay kee-shee-wah-tay.
(Weesakayjaak once, he went fishing. He was getting really hungry.)
O-gee-waa-bah-maan Misko-tay-sheens ay-kee-sho-shich a-sin-nee-kaang.
(He saw the Turtle warming itself on the rock.)
A-mee-o-maa waysh-kuch Misko-tay-sheens ka-ween o-gee-a-yaa-seen o-waa-kaa-i-gun.
(At this time a long time ago, Turtle did not have his house or shell.)
A-wih-ya-shee-shug, bin-nay-sheens-suhg o-wee-a-moh-waan ay-noo-koh-sich ay-mino-poh-koh-sich.
(Animals and birds always wanted to eat him because he was soft and good to eat.)
Misko-tay-sheens o-gee-waa-ba-maan Nin-gik ay-pee-shaa-nich.
(Turtle saw Otter approach.)
Ka-shi-shay-goh-bah-nooch a-naa-ming a-sin-nee-kaang.
(He crawled under a rock.)
Kee-say-kih-zih.
(He was scared.)
Wee-sa-kay-jaak o-gee-waa-bun-daan ka-kee-i-zhi-way-bung.
(Weesakayjaak saw what happened.)
O-gee-koh-baa-tayn-nih-maan Misko-tay-sheen.
(He felt sorry for Turtle.)

"Kih-say-kihs nah?" Wee-sa-kay-jaak kah-kway-tway.
("Are you scared?" Weesakayjaak asked.)
"Ah-hih, nih-say-kihs, bih-saam nih-mino-poh-koos,"
I-kit-toh Misko-tay-sheens.
("Yes, I'm scared, I taste too good," said Turtle.)
"Am-bay kah-wee-cheen, ninga-o-shi-doon waa-ka-i-gun
chi-i-zhi-taa-yun. A-zhas-kih ninga-a-toon kih-wee-won-
nong, kih-tig-won, kih-kaad-don, kih-o-soh, kih-taa a-
toon-nun been-dig a-way-nayn ay-wee a-mih-goh-yun."
("Come here, I'll help you, I'll build you a house. I'll put
mud on your body, your head, your legs, your tail; you can
put them inside whenever someone wants to eat you.")
Ween-gay Misko-tay-sheens gee-mino-wayn-dum kah-gee-
too-tung Wee-sa-kay-jaak.
(Turtle was very pleased with what Weesakayjaak did.)
O-gee-ween-dah-moh-waan ah-neen-dih Wee-sa-kay-jaak
chi tay-bih-naach neem-boh gee-gons-sun.
(He told Weesakayjaak where to find lots of fish.)
A-mee-way-tush ay-on-chi-gee-ah-yaach Misko-tay-sheens
o-waa-ka-i-gun.
(That is why Turtle got his house.)

One of the other characters that frequently appeared in their
stories was a spirit creature called Cha-kaa-bayns. He was known
to be a great hunter and carried a bow and arrow. Us children always wanted to be like him. At night during the winter when we
were ready to go to sleep, we heard the crack of the trees. Sometimes it was so cold outside that the trees made loud sounds as if
they were falling apart. Our parents would tell us that these
sounds were Cha-kaa-bayns hunting in the woods with his bow
and arrow. The cracking sound came from one his arrows as it

missed an animal and hit a tree. The next morning, I would wake
up and go outside to look at the trees to see Cha-kaa-bayns's
arrow. I never did find one.

Our parents told us that when the ice on the lake or the river
cracked and made loud noises, it was Cha-kaa-bayns under the
ice fighting a big fish like a sturgeon. It could also be him chasing
and catching an evil spirit or the water serpent under the ice. The
cracking sound would be his axe or spear hitting the ice and echo-
ing over the lake or the river. At night during the winter we heard
all types of adventures and we begged our parents to hear more
at-soh-kaa-nun every night.

The at-soh-kaa-nun scared us so much that we never ventured
out from our log cabin alone without one of our parents. When
we did, we stayed close to our Mom and Dad. There were stories
of evil spirits that took children away, especially ones who didn't
listen, who didn't follow instructions, and who always misbe-
haved. We never got lost in the wilderness because we were so
afraid. We never had serious accidents because we followed instructions. We were always careful. We knew what happened to
Weeshakayjaak. We didn't want that to happen to us.

Our Mom and Dad also told us stories of our grandfather.
Our father's father used to deliver mail for the Hudson's Bay
Company during winter. He had his toboggan full of mail and
delivered it to the other reserves in the region: Fort Hope,
Landsdowne House, and Webique. He had a dog team to pull
his toboggan. This happened before the bush planes arrived in
the territory. He was old and he even told us about the time the
people had flintlock guns. Mom and Dad had plenty of stories
about grandfather.

One of grandfather's stories told to us by our Mom was the
time he witnessed the partridge social dance. He happened to be
checking his traps and snares one day. The trees were covered with

snow. The day was nice and calm with no wind. He noticed some snow falling from the spruce tree stand he was approaching. He wondered why the snow would be falling from certain trees in a particular area. He crept up to the tree stand. He saw a bunch of partridge sitting on spruce branches and moving around to get a better view of the ground. On the ground the snow was packed down by a group of partridge dancing. They were doing the round dance. The dancers went from left to right in a circle. They must have been from the Anishinaabay Nation. Grandfather watched them for a while and slowly backed away.

We didn't have any electricity. At night we would light a kerosene lamp. It had a bulbous base made out of clear crystal. Dad filled it up with the kerosene gas and we could see it through the crystal. The gas soaked a wick that was inside the base and went through a slanted hole. We saw the top part of the wick and it was adjusted by a small knob on the side. The wick is lit with a match. The flame is controlled by turning the knob. The flame was protected by a long glass covering that had openings at both ends. If you wanted it to be bright, the wick is let out more; if you wanted low lighting, the knob is turned down; if you wanted to get romantic ... EEEEEE!

These were the times when we could afford kerosene. When we had no gas for the lamp we went to the candle. At times we ran out of candles, so we went to plan C. We used a button for a lamp. A button is rolled up in a piece of cloth which is twisted into a tight bun. The cloth is tied with a piece of string. The end piece of the cloth is now the wick. The covered button is then placed in a small dish full of animal fat or lard. The animal fat or lard has been melted down to oil. The button is soaking wet and now it floats on top of the oil. The cloth is lit with a match and would give us light. We woke up the next morning with our nostrils full of black soot.

We had running water in that I would run down to the lake to get water. During the winter months, a full moon was scary. I would have to go out onto the ice to the water hole that was chiseled out of the lake by our Dad. It would be frozen around the water hole and it had to be chiseled out at times. There was always a chisel or an axe at the water hole. In one of the empty pails we brought a toy-bay-gun (saucepan) to dip into the water hole. I filled up the water pails with haste as I looked out for the evil spirit Ween-dih-go or roaming may-in-gun-ug (wolves).

I was also scared of the moon that took a little boy with two pails. In this story, the moon felt sorry for a boy as he was an orphan who was often beaten by a bad uncle. The boy went down to the water hole on the lake one night during the winter. The boy looked up to the moon and he started crying. A beam of light came down from the moon and took him away. We were told if we looked up at a full moon, we could be the boy with two pails of water. I knew the moon wouldn't take me because I have two loving and protective parents. But I still scurried off the ice with my two full pails of water.

The evil spirit Wendigo was always said to be present in the wilderness. He ate people. He was always hungry and could never be full. He appeared most in the winter when it was cold. That was why we always stayed close by to our Mom and why we never wandered off. We didn't want to be eaten.

Another character we were always afraid of was Pah-kak, the flying skeleton with long black hair. It is said that it flies around in the air with its long, flowing hair hanging down. It always was screaming an awful howl. It is said that if anyone sees it, or even hears the howl, that that person is going to live a long life. Our Mom told us one of her brothers had heard it and he lived a long life.

These stories with their characters kept us in check. They made sure that we were careful when outside in the bush or on the water and that we did not misbehave. Instead of our Mom and Dad watching over us, we had stories to keep us in line. They were our teachers.

Our Dad was home most of the time during our stay at Washi Lake in winter. We always followed him around camp. I stood at his side while he chopped the firewood. The wood is cut with a buck saw into short firewood. Dad split the wood with an axe with great skill. The wood is dried spruce, poplar, cedar, and birch. In winter we followed him into the bush, him pulling us on the empty toboggan. The silent forest went by us while we were being pulled along. The trail is hard packed by Dad's snowshoes and by the frequent use of it. The trees are cut down using the buck saw and the axe. The branches are knocked off with the swift swing of the axe and the tree is cut to the height of about eight feet. Dad carries the tree on his shoulder to the toboggan. He does this a number of times and each time he places the trees on the toboggan. After a nice pile of trees are on, they are tied to the toboggan with ropes from the sides. We jumped on the logs and rode them all the way home. Dad is at the front using a long rope to pull us and the wood. I anticipated the little hills that were on the trail. The toboggan rises up for a while until the front of it came crashing down hard. Us Ojibway invented the rollercoaster.

Riding along on top of the firewood, we were surrounded by snow that muffled the sound of our movement. Sometimes we heard the quee-queesh-shug (grey jays), making a huge ruckus somewhere in the forest. We asked our Dad what they were doing. He said the birds were laughing and teasing an owl. The owl would be sitting on a branch trying to get some sleep after a long night of hunting. The grey jays were calling others to join in the fun.

The logs are taken off at a sawhorse structure that was built by tying two logs together at the ends with the top part of the logs making a V shape. Another one is about five feet away. The two parts are joined by a board along each side to fortify it. A log is placed on top of the sawhorse to be cut with a buck saw. I sat on top of the log that was being cut into firewood. The other logs were placed standing up, leaning on a nearby tree. They waited. The cut firewood is placed on top of a chopping block. I watched Dad split the wood. One half of the split wood is laid on the chopping block and it is cut into four thinner pieces for kindling. He held up the other half of firewood on a slant placed on the chopping block. The edge part is cut into curled wood chips and these were used for fire starters. They burned quickly when a lit match was held to them, and the thinner pieces were placed on top of them until they caught on fire. The bigger pieces of firewood were then put in when the fire started to get going in the stove. The woodstove was used for warmth and cooking.

There was a lid on top of the woodstove that was opened for the wood to be put in. In the front of the stove near the bottom, there is a valve that was used to control how much heat was needed. It is opened wide to generate more air flow going into the stove and to create more heat. It is closed to stop the air flow and this generated less heat. The little woodstove would have red glowing cheeks on its sides when the valve was fully opened. The top lid would dance when the stove was going full blast. It would calm down when the valve was closed.

We always had tea. The kettle full of water is placed on top of the stove. Steam ran out of the front spout and moved the top lid of the kettle up and down. The water was boiled, and we added loose tea leaves when we were poor or tea bags when we had extra money. At about this time the bannock is ready. This was our bread. Mom and Dad mixed flour with baking soda and added the right amount of melted lard at the correct temperature to the dry mixture. This made the dough that was placed on a greased frying pan. This was also placed on the stove for it to bake. The dough was flipped over for the other side to cook. For a treat, Mom and Dad added raisins to the mixture. It is steaming hot when a piece is ready for us. We slathered our bannock with lard and it melted inside the dough. Sugar, lots of it, goes into our cups. The bannock is dunked into our tea, leaving a greasy oil slick. This was a treat.

Choo-chup (oatmeal) was a main staple for us when we travelled far distances. In winter we pulled up along the shore and made a quick fire. An ice hole is chopped out of the lake or river to get water to boil for tea. The water boils in the kettle over the fire and tea is added. We each get a cup and the tea is added along with a handful of oats. Sugar is dumped in and it is mixed with the oats. The last thing we add is a chunk of frozen lard. We get a piece of frozen bannock and we dunked it into the choo-chup. It is filling. We put everything away on the toboggan and away we went.

Once we were travelling in our toboggan with all our belongings. We were heading down to our spring camp to wait out the ice breakup. Stopping along the river just before it got dark, we made an overnight camp with no tent. Dad made a huge fire outside. We were going to sleep under the stars. The dogs were tied up. The roaring fire threw sparks up into the dark sky. Tea was being made over the fire, in the kettle. The bannock was placed in the frying pan and it was baked with hot coals beneath it. Dad had picked frozen cranberries along the shoreline and they were boiling in a saucepan beside the fire. When the cranberries were cooked, sugar was added to them. We had a feast that night. The

bannock was being dunked into the tea. We were eating our cranberries when Dad started choking. He couldn't stop. We got wor-
ried. He struggled to breathe and gasped for air. He gulped down
some tea and that helped. The bannock went down the wrong
way. There was a moment of silence after that.

Mom finally said "Gaa-shug!" This means someone who is
greedy. We laughed.

CHAPTER 9

Paa-tih-goh-seeng
(Spring camp)

In late winter we put away the toboggan and brought out the ish-pih-gun-nay (sleigh with high runners). The ish-pih-gun-nay has two low, narrow boards that are attached with two higher boards. The bottom boards are the runners as they touch the ground. There are wooden slats that cover the top runners that start near the front and go to the back. The upper runners are attached to the lower ones with short wooden pegs nailed into the runners. The runners are made out of a certain type of birch tree. These birch trees are found in areas where there is moisture in the ground. The birch tree that grows straight without any knots is ideal. This ensures that the grains in the trees will be straight. The tree is cut down and it is cut again to about eight feet in length. The tree is split using dried wood pegs cut into wedges. The two halves are split again to make four parts. The four pieces of birch are then formed into rough flat runners for the sleigh. The axe is used for this process. The runners are brought back to the camp to be shaved into smooth flat runners. The lower flat runners are bent up and attached to the upper straight runners using nails. Ropes are attached at certain intervals on the side of the sleigh. These ropes tied our belongings down when we were travelling.

The sleigh is used to travel to our Paa-tih-goh-seeng (spring camp) as the weather starts to warm up in the early spring.

The days start to get longer in early spring. We spent the winter on Washi Lake. The weather tells us when it is time to move. The snow starts to melt. Brown patches of ground appear, especially along the north shore. Our Dad starts to prepare for the move to our spring camp. It is situated down the river from Washi Lake. We go by rapids and falls, with some still frozen and some open. Dad gets the sleigh ready by turning it over so that the bottom runners are exposed. He puts flattened stove pipes over the runners. These are old stove pipes and they are nailed onto the runners. The sleigh is turned over and it slides back and forth with ease on the snow. The sleigh will now go smoother over the ice on the lakes and river. The dogs know that something is up. They start to whine in low voices.

The next thing to do was to turn over the sixteen-foot freighter canvas canoe. Last fall it was placed high above the ground between two wood stands that held it up. The canoe is placed upright on the sleigh. The ropes from the sleigh are tied over the canoe to keep it in place. The dogs start to move around, stretching, yawning, and looking at our Dad expectantly.

With the canoe secured, Dad loads our gear into it: the boat motor, gas tank, ten-gallon gas drum, and the paddles. He then loads the various traps he will be using for the spring trapping. The woodstove, along with the pipes, also goes in the back. The canvas tent is packed also. The middle part of the canoe is where our Mom, Jerry, and I will sit. Back packs full of our blankets and clothes are used for our seats. Close by us will be the mee-jih-moh-wus (food box), full of food for the journey. Our cooking utensils are placed in a different canvas bag. There is always the twenty-five-pound bag of flour. Somewhere in the pile is Mom's sewing kit. Waa-boh-waan is a large cover blanket full of goose down that she had made, and this was placed over us for the journey. The front of the canoe is loaded with the water pails, axes, chisels, and buck saw.

Our four dogs are now jumping and howling as they see our Dad bring the dog harness out. The harness is attached to the sleigh and laid out on the ground. The back harness is near the sleigh, two harnesses are side-by-side in the middle, and there is the front harness for the lead dog. Dad approaches the dogs and they are standing on their hind legs straining their leash. One of our dogs was named Hoss. He was the strong silent type as he never showed any emotion. Our Dad harnesses him at the back of the harness, near the front of the sleigh. A strong dog was needed there so he can pull the sleigh left or right as needed. Next were the two working dogs that were harnessed side-by-side in the middle. Their names were August and Chop Chop. They were so excited to leave that Dad had a hard time putting them on their harness. The lead dog, Chuck, is most happy to get moving. Chuck is the lead dog because he is the smartest and listens to the commands given by our Dad. He would give them commands like pay-kaach (slow down), kih-bih-cheen (stop), and kay-nih-gohk (go hard). They were able to understand Anishinaabaymowin, the Anishinaabay language. This was all done before the sun came up.

Before every spring trip we always waited for our Mom. The dogs are straining in their harness and waiting for the word, maa-chaan! (go!), from Dad. We waited to call out to our Mom to hurry. The whole operation was ready to go but Mom is still up at the log cabin. She finally came out without saying a word and got in the canoe. We were off to our destination. The dogs put all their strength into their harness and slowly moved us into motion. Dad helps to pull the sleigh until the dogs are moving the sleigh on their own. You could hear their yelps and howling when they got started before they settled into a steady run. The sleigh slides steadily on the smooth ice. We saw the eastern horizon blazed with orange, red, yellow, purple, and pink colours before the sun came over the trees. There is always a moment of stillness, a moment of caution, before the sun made its appearance. We travelled close to the shoreline. The early morning is cold. The snow melts off the ice. Mid-day brings the warm sun and the slush. The slush slows down the sleigh as the runners get wet. We travelled on the south shore. The sun didn't shine there with the trees in the way.

Mom places us in the middle of the canoe and covers us in the waa-boh-waan. She sits with us. Dad usually ran with the dogs for a while and then would jump on the back of the sleigh, giving encouragement to the dogs. We rode along the lakes and river in the canoe on top of the sleigh. We glide through the snow and ice in silence. We took our lunch break when the sun was high in the sky.

We stopped for lunch along the shoreline. A fire is made, water is put in the tea kettle, and the tea kettle is put on the fire. The mee-jih-moh-wush is taken out. The cups, sugar, lard, and oats are ready for the tea. The bannock is frozen. The cups have the tea in them, and we add the sugar, oats, and lard. The frozen bannock is slathered with lard and it's dunked in the choo-chup. The dogs rest for a moment after getting some water and food. We are soon on our way. At this time of the year the wind picks up during the day and blows the dead leaves around. The wind tumbles brown leaves along the surface of the ice. I follow a brown leaf tumbling along the ice as it is being blown by the wind. I still wonder if that leaf is still moving, even to this day.

We follow the shoreline to our destination. The Albany River is still frozen. Some smaller rapids are still frozen. The bigger falls are open due to the fast-moving water. We bypass the open water by going over the portage. The afternoon starts to get cold as the sun gets lower in the sky. We set up an overnight camp along the river. The dogs are tied to some trees and given food and water. They are tired from the journey. Mom and Dad set up the canvas tent. The woodstove is placed inside the tent. The floor in the tent is covered with spruce boughs for insulation and comfort. Our blankets are laid out over the boughs and our waa-boh-waan is placed over the blankets. The stove soon heats up the tent, a meal is made, and we fall asleep. The next morning, we are up and moving before the sun.

We reach the Paa-tih-goh-seeng in the afternoon. It is situated on the north shore of the Albany River. We wait for breakup of the ice here. The dogs are tied up, fed, and given water. They soon fall asleep. There is a wooden frame for the tent. There are six logs, one on top of each other, that runs along the perimeter where the tent is going to be placed. The front faces the east with a door cut out of it. Tripod poles are set up at the front and back of the wooden structure. A long pole is placed between the two tripods. The tent is hung on the long pole with ropes that are tied in intervals along the pole. The sides of the tent have long ropes that are tied to wooden stakes in the ground. They are pulled tight to shape the tent over the wooden structure. The bottom sides of the tent are nailed to the logs around the tent. These logs make the tent higher for us inside. The snow is removed from inside the log frame. We have a wooden floor inside so that we didn't have to sleep on the bare ground. This time we do not have to use the spruce boughs.

Dad puts the stove pipes together and they are placed through a hole in the top of the tent. The hole is made big enough to attach a round steel plate with a hole in it where the stove pipe will go through. This steel plate protects the canvas cloth from catching fire when the stove pipes get hot. We put all our belongings inside the tent after the stove is lit. The canoe is placed above the ground between the two wood braces to dry it out. The sleigh is placed against the tree to keep the runners off the ground. The dog harness is placed on top of the wooden platform that stands outside to keep things off the ground. Moose and beaver meat are also placed on top of the wooden platform to keep it away from the dogs. The traps are put there too. The guns are placed inside the tent in the corner far away from the stove and from us.

The stove is on all day and night as it is still cold outside. To keep the fire going all night, Dad puts in dry birch logs and turns down the valve. Slowly everyone settles down; we are warm, full, tired, and happy to be at Paa-tih-goh-seeng. We sleep and dream warm all night.

This place is situated near a waterfall that is up the river towards Washi Lake. Washi Lake is far up the river from us now. Below us, down the river, is the reserve community Ogoki Post. We are about a day away from the reserve by canoe. Our camp is on a point and we can see the frozen river going downstream and disappearing around the bend. Across from our camp on the south shore there is a small river that meets the Albany River. This small river is also called Paa-tih-goh-seeng. We will go up the Paa-tih-goh-seeng when the river thaws. This river almost runs parallel up the Albany River on the south side. This small river has plenty of muskrats and beaver to trap and snare.

Down the river from our camp on the north shore there is a small creek that runs into the Albany River. Our Dad walks on his snowshoes with his traps and snare wire inside his packsack. At this time of the year he goes up the creek without a paddle. He takes his axe and sets various traps and snares in places. Along the way Dad looks for tracks from rabbits, mink, marten, and otter. The snare wire is mainly for rabbits and beavers. Rabbits are snared using strong brass wire. The beavers are snared using a stronger wire. Both wires are long enough to go around a strong, dry stick, but the beaver needs a thicker stick. One end of the wire is twisted into a teardrop loop and the other end is pushed through it. For the rabbit, the snare is sized using the shape of a tight fist. The beaver snare is a little larger. Beavers have big heads.

Dad sets Waa-boo-zoog (rabbit) snares along the river where there is a lot of track activity. The snow tracks tell him where the main trail used by the rabbits is. This is where he sets the snare. A dry, solid stick is used to tie one end of the snare. The snare wire has already been looped to the size of the rabbit's head. This is set right over the rabbit trail. The stick is stuck in the ground. Little dry sticks are placed on both sides of the snare to guide the rabbit to run through the snare. While the rabbit is moving it gets caught in the snare and it strangles itself quickly by trying to get away. Dad brings back a few rabbits when he checks the traps after a few days. The rabbits are frozen solid in his packsack when he arrives. The rabbits are then thawed out and their hide is taken off. Their hide is placed on a wooden stretcher and pulled inside out. Rabbit skin hats and blankets are made with them.

Waa-boo-zoog make snow-packed running trails just days before a snowstorm. They spread out their paws to pack down the snow. This helps to make their trails harder. The snow will soon fall and covers the trail. Whenever a fox or marten chases them after the snowfall, the rabbits know where the trail is and follow it back to their holes. The animals chasing them do not know where the hard-packed snow is. Instead they run through the deep snow and are slowed down. This is how the rabbit gets away and the fox and marten stay hungry.

Dad sets the traps for marten, mink, and otter wherever he sees active signs in the snow and on the ice. He comes to a beaver dam and behind that is the house. In front of the house, a pile of branches sticks out of the ice. This is the food that the beaver has used for the winter. The pond behind the dam is still frozen and hard enough to walk on. There will be a family of beavers living inside the house that include the parents, a couple of yearlings, and maybe a two-year-old. On both sides of the food pile the ice is thin. Looking through the ice, there are a lot of air bubbles below the ice. This indicates that the beaver is coming and going from the tunnel of the house and the food pile. They get the wood that is underwater and take it back to the house to eat. You can also fall through the ice if you step in this spot. But this is where you break through the ice with the axe to set the snare for the beaver.

The ice is broken with the axe. It floats in the open water and is cleared using the saucepan. If there is no saucepan Dad uses his bare hands to scoop out the ice from the cold water. The cleared opening is now ready to set the snare. A curved stick is shoved into the beaver house to find the entrance under the water. A straight stick is pushed under the water until it hits the bottom. The point where the water touches the stick is noted and it is moved from one side of the ice hole to the other side. The poking will tell you where the stick went in deeper as it touched the ground under water. This tells you where the tunnel is located. Sticks are placed where the top parts of the tunnel are. These are posts to make sure the beaver is guided to go through them.

The beaver snares are prepared in the tent beforehand. The wire is twisted at one end by looping the wire onto itself a number of times to create a teardrop hole. The other end will be passed through the hole to make the snare. Dad takes out the prepared snare and passes the straight end through the hole. The straight end is then twisted onto the dry stick that will stick out of the ice hole. The thicker end of this stick is cut by using the axe to sharpen its end. The sharpened end is stuck into the ground underwater. The snare wire is placed above this end and it hangs where the underwater tunnel is. Other sticks are placed on both sides of the guideposts to make a gate-like structure. The beaver gets snared underwater and quickly strangles itself. It drowns and the stick stuck in the ground prevents it from being dragged away. This is done to the other entrance on the other side of the food pile. The traps and snares are checked every few days.

The beaver that is caught is underwater and the ice needs to be chopped out. It is taken out of the water and the snare is taken off. The snare is reset and placed back in the water to catch the next one. Dad puts the beaver on the sleigh with all the other trapped animals. They are all frozen. The animals are brought back and put inside the tent to thaw out. The animals are skinned in various ways. The beaver pelt is taken off using a sharp up-turned blade. The meat and fat are removed from the hide. The beaver carcass is then cleaned by gutting out the entrails. These are thrown outside for the quee-queesh-shug (whisky jacks) to eat. They are also known as the grey jay.

The beaver is cooked by cutting it up and putting it in water to make stew. Oats are added to it. See-boyh (dumplings) are made and added to the stew. It is very tasty. The meat that was not cooked is placed outside on top of a wooden structure we call tay-saa-quay-gun. This platform is made with strong, tall saplings. They are tied together near the top and are stood up to form a teepee-like structure. The supporting sticks have other shorter sticks tied to them to make the platform. These are above the ground. The moose, beaver and other carcasses are placed here to be frozen. This was our outdoor refrigerator. Of course, the quee-queesh-shug always came around our camp to see what there was to eat. The black and white colouring on their body makes them stand out against the white snow. The only place they are found is in the northern boreal forest.

The quee-queesh-shug would pick off the meat from our platforms. Once I set a small leg-hold trap for them. I checked the trap one morning and it had been sprung but there was no quee-queesh there. On the tongue of the trap there was the remaining bill of a quee-queesh. I never told my parents about this. That was the end of my trapping career. I felt bad after that as I knew I did something wrong. To appease the Quee-queesh Nation I acknowledge them.

CHAPTER 10

Moonz-oog
(Moose)

Our Dad was a great provider. He was also a great hunter. Once Mom told me a story about the time when they were out hunting in a canoe and Dad killed a moonz (moose) that he couldn't see.

They were following a narrow point when they spotted a moose. It was just coming out of the bush. The moose saw the canoe and went back into the bush. It then walked along the shore on the other side of the point. Dad stood up at the back of the canoe and fired the .30-30 rifle into the direction of where the moose was. They turned the corner at the point and the moose was found lying close to the shore. He hit the moose with a shot behind the ear. They had many great meals from the kill. The best part of a moose is the nostril and the tongue. They didn't tell us that until we were adults. The meat is so soft when cooked properly over an open fire outside. This is the only way to cook moose.

There are a number of ways to hunt moonz-oog. In the fall the moose are rutting. This is their mating season. The male moose fight each other using their huge antlers for the right to mate the female. To entice the male moose to come out of the bush you make the sounds of a female moose. Dad used to pour water into the lake, pond, or stream using a tin can to make the sound of a female moose peeing. Another way to entice them out was to use a female moose call. Dad would put his hands out in front of his mouth and call. The sound he made sounded like "huu-uuh!" This is the female call that is soft and enticing that drives the male moose mad at this time of the year. The male moose runs into the open to show off his mighty antlers. A moose hunter now has a chance to get the moose.

During winter our Dad told us that the best time to hunt a moose is when there is a storm. The wind has to be facing you so that the moose does not catch your scent. The moose will also not hear any noise that you might make in the bush when it is windy. You also have to remember to wear parkas and pants that are cloth, so they won't make scratching noises when hitting branches. Moose tracks are easy to follow in the winter. The front hooves leave marks in the snow to tell you the direction they are going.

When the moose is shot the hide is skinned off. The moose is then quartered in the snow. The hot blood turns the snow deep red. The moose parts are wrapped in the moose hide and dragged back to camp by hand, by the dogs, or by using the toboggan. The meat is then placed on the tay-saa-quay-gun, the wooden platform outside our camp.

The most important part of the moose for us is the hide. Neegan in-nayn-dum-moh-win means "the leading thought," and this is what the women think of the hide when a moose is killed. The hide is used to make all kinds of clothes for everyone in our family. Mom made moccasins for us that were used for snowshoeing. There were also beaded moccasins made for tourists that ordered them. We rarely saw Mom make moose hide jackets with beads and fringes because these were made for people that were special or were in politics. She also made mittens and vests out of tanned moose hide. The men who killed the moose had to be careful while skinning the moose hide so that there were no holes.

The moose hide is tanned by braining the hide. This means that the brain of the moose will be used as a softening agent. This is a process that the Anishinaabayg have been using for centuries. There is no harmful chemical used in the process. It is done using all-natural products. The hair of the moose is taken off using a sharp knife with a curved end. The meat and fat are also taken off using this knife. The hide is thick at this point. It will be scraped to a thin, nearly transparent raw hide. The thick hide is sewn into a large rectangular wooden frame. The frame has four long poles nailed together to form the rectangle. The four corners have shorter poles nailed to them so that the frame holds its shape. A long string with a big needle is pulled through the hide and it is placed over the long pole of the frame. The needle is returned to the edge of the moose hide and pulled through the hide again. This is repeated until the whole hide is sewn on the inside part of the wooden frame.

The hide is then tightened to the frame until it is taut. The frame is left outside in winter so that the hide will freeze. Very early in the morning, before the sun comes up, Dad is outside scraping the moose hide. He uses an axe with a short handle that he made especially for this process: the regular axe handle is taken out and replaced with a shortened handle made of birch. The axe head has a long horizontal hole where the original handle was. A birch handle is fashioned and shoved through the hole. Now both sides of the axe have handles. The handles are bent towards each other and they are tied together to create one handle. It sticks out of the side of the axe, which is used as a scraper. The blade is very sharp.

Dad scrapes the frozen moose hide by pressing on the axe head while pulling down the wooden handle. The scrapes produce curls of hide that fall down to the ground. The whole hide is done this way, on both sides. The scraping makes the hide transparent. The hide is then much thinner. It is taken off the stretcher and brought inside our tent to thaw out. When it becomes thawed it is pliable.

At this stage, the hide is then placed in a tub of cold water. It is time to make moose hide string or webbings for snowshoes. Mom and Dad do this by cutting the hide into a long string. Dad takes a sharp knife and starts by cutting into the outside edge of the wet hide. Mom holds out the hide where the cuts are going to be made. This spreads the hide and makes the cutting easier. Dad uses his thumb as a guide to make a constant thickness to the string. The thinner string is going to be used for the front and back ends of the snowshoes. The middle part of the snowshoe will have thicker moose hide string as this is where the snowshoe will take the most pounding from the feet.

The traditional way of tanning moose hide has been done for centuries by knowledgeable Anishinaabay. When the hide is going to be used for clothing, there is the tanning process that uses the whole brain of the moose. The hide is taken out of the tub and hung up to dry. While this is happening, the brain is cooked in a pot with water until it bubbles. It is then taken out and allowed to cool off. Do not eat the brain. The brain solution is now ready to be placed on both sides of the dried moose hide. The brain solution is then left on the hide for a couple of days to start its work. It settles into the hide by slowly embedding itself onto the surface. The brain has acid in it that helps to soften the hide. Though the brain is on the hide, it needs to go in deeper into the hide to get into all the fibres. The hide is not placed in water at this stage as the brain will wash off. This is when the first smoking needs to be done.

The wood used is pee-kih-chees-sug, dried wood found in dead stumps. It is collected and placed in a pail. The moose hide is folded in half and sewn together only at the top and along the side. The bottom part of the hide is left open. A canvas skirt is sewn around the bottom opening. The hide with its skirt is hoisted up by rope and tied to a pole that is nailed between two trees. The pail of pee-kih-chees-sug is then placed over the canvas skirt. The pee-kih-chees-sug is then lit with only the smoke allowed to come up the skirt and the hide. You don't want open flames coming from the pee-kih-chees-sug or you will fry the moose brain and ruin the hide. You don't want fried moose brain on your new jacket.

The smoke permeates into the hide. When the heat from the smoke of the pee-kih-chees-sug goes through the hide, the hide starts to sweat as its pores open up. As the pores open, the moose brain seeps further into the hide. This process is done outside so that you do not get smoked out and have your own pores open up. The hide is then taken inside when the first smoking is finished. It is stiff as a board. It is left alone for a couple of days so that the brain can settle into the hide further and soften the fibres inside. After a couple of days, the hide is placed in a tub of tent-temperature water. The brain won't wash off of the hide now as it is trapped deep inside. The hide becomes soft again as it is in the water. The next stage is to take the hide out of the water and squeeze it dry. This is done by having two people twisting the hide between them. One person twists the hide to the left while the other person twists it to the right. The water is taken out of the hide until it becomes soft.

To make the hide even softer, two people stretch it beside a hot stove. As the hide is still damp this helps it to dry out even more. At this point the brain solution has broken down the moose hide fibres. Pulling the hide beside the stove tears the fibres even more to make the hide supple. It also makes the hide turn white in colour. Now the clothes our Mom will make will be white; the moose hide jacket, the moccasins, and the mitts will all be white. Wearing these, you could blend into the snow and no one will see where you are. The hide is given a second smoking, and this turns the hide a tan colour. The smell of wood smoke stays in the clothes for years. This smell tells you the hide was tanned using the traditional method.

The beaver hides are also stretched this way. Smaller frames are used to tie the beaver hides. The hides are sewn onto the wood frames using a big needle with strong twine. The outside edges of the hide have the needle pulled through and then the twine is pulled over the wood frame. The beaver pelt is sewn onto the frame and it is tightened to make it taut. The pelt in the frame is hung on tree branches to keep it off the ground. The beaver pelts are left outside to freeze overnight. Dad scrapes off the side where the meat and fat were. The hide is now smooth and white. The hides are taken inside to thaw out. The beaver hide is then dry and taken off the frame. Each pelt is then rolled up and put into a sack. Mom makes clothes from them or Dad sells them to traders. Their fur is soft like new snow.

We wait for the snow to melt. The days are longer now, and the sun melts the snow from the ground. The ice starts to melt on the river. There is now open water in the middle of the river. This gets wider as the days get warmer. The first sign of spring is when the geese come back. They land on the open water and sit on the edge of the ice. Dad gets ducks and geese by shooting them with the shotgun. The water gets higher on the river and soon breaks up the ice holding onto the shoreline. The smaller tributaries flood the Albany River and raise the water level further still. This lifts the remaining ice off the shore and the breakup begins.

Huge chunks of ice float by our front yard. They look like gigantic ships passing, hurrying down the river. They shove the smaller ones up onto the shoreline. In their haste some submerge into the fast-moving water but sooner or later they reappear down the river. Sometimes they jump up from the water and turn over making a big splash. When one passes there is always another one to take its place. The ice chunks pushed up into the shoreline break trees and brush. They lie there, dying a slow death. Little icicles break off the body of the icebergs, making tinkling sounds. This happens all day and all night. We heard the movement of the ice and river while we were falling asleep in the tent with the wood stove keeping us warm. We tried to fall asleep, but we had persuaded Mom and Dad to tell us a story. How can anyone sleep when you heard about water serpents and evil ween-dih-goog (spirits)? I often wonder why we weren't nervous all the time after growing up hearing those terrible stories. Maybe we were.

CHAPTER 11

Shaa-gun-naa-shee-shug
(People who don't tell the truth)

The breakup lasts for a while as the ice chunks get smaller and fewer. The ice pushed up onto the shore sits motionless and slowly dying until it takes its last breath as an ice form. It melts. It becomes part of the river. It becomes a different creation.

It was time for spring trapping. The canoe is turned over. The wooden sleigh is stood up against a tree to wait for the next winter. Kih-chi Zii-bii (the Big River), the Albany River, is high and the water is running fast. The smaller rivers empty into the big river and it's time to go up them in the canoe. The canoe is filled up with all our gear: tent, stove, food box, traps, snares, axe, saw, paddles, gas containers, gas tank, guns, pack sacks full of clothes and blankets. We go up the creek with our canoe using a small outdoor motor. There will be rapids and small falls to portage. The travel on these small rivers is still dangerous as the water is high and it's still cold outside. The dogs are left on their leash and tied up at the main spring camp. We cannot take them with us because the water that they would have to cross on the shore will be too cold.

We go up the river to where we are going to trap beaver and muskrat. It is early morning and it's cold. We find floating logs that are stuck on the banks of the river. These logs have muskrat droppings on them telling us that this log is a feeding place. Mom or Dad takes an axe and starts chopping on top of the log. Large chunks of wood are taken off until there is a smooth place big enough for a small leg-hold trap to set there. The trap is opened and it has a short chain with a steel ring at the end. The ring is nailed into the log. The muskrat will step on the log and step on the trap. It will then fall into the water to get away and it will eventually drown. Mom and Dad do this on both sides of the river because it is not wide.

Trapping beaver in spring is more work than it is trapping beaver in winter. The beaver houses are found along the river and the size of them will determine if there are at least two big beaver living in them. There will also be a couple of yearlings in every house. A large number of tree saplings sticking out of the water tells us there will be lots of beaver there. The beaver houses are situated along the shoreline. There are smooth mud slides made by the beavers near the house where they have gone into the bush to get trees for food. The slides are a good place to put the beaver traps.

These traps are a bit bigger than the ones used for muskrat. There are two handles on the trap. The trap is opened with the two blades spread apart. There is a long, thin steel clip put over one of the blades of the trap and it is attached to a tongue that holds the trap open. When the tongue is stepped on, the trap closes tightly on the leg. The trap has a long chain attached to one end of the handles. The chain has a ring at the end of it. This ring is pushed over the top end of a dry pole until it gets stuck near the bottom of the thick end of it. The bottom part of the stick has been chopped into a point to stick into the mud. The ring is also nailed into the stick to keep it in place. The dry pole is about six to eight feet long so it can be seen sticking out of the water when the beaver is caught. The trap has heavy rocks tied to the stick. There is a stick from a poplar tree that is placed on land near where the trap is set. On this stick Dad smears beaver castor as bait. This musk attracts the female as it is mating season. The male beaver is attracted to it too as it tells him there might be another male around. The trap, the pole, and the rocks are all set in front of the stick. As the beaver approaches the stick, it will step on the trap and it will pull the whole apparatus into the water. The rocks are used as anchors to hold the beaver down under water. It drowns the beaver and the pole sticking out of the water shows where the beaver is. If the stick is found far from the original setting, then it's a big beaver. We call it kih-chi keen-nih-boh-jih-gun.

The beaver castors are taken out when the beavers are cleaned. They are hung out to dry. The castors are also sold to the Hudson's Bay Company. They are used in the making of perfume and cologne. Some castors are small and some are big. Go figure.

The beaver snares are set in the entrances of the beaver house. The snares are placed on long poles and they, too, have rocks attached to them for weights. All the traps and snares are set along both sides of the small river. There are parts of the river where there is no current, so Mom and Dad have to paddle there. Mom sits at the front of the canoe. Dad sits at the back paddling and steering the canoe. He drives the paddle into the water and gives it a twist on the pull up to steer the canoe in a straight line. He repeats this motion for every stroke. There is a distinct sound of *chomp* when the paddle goes into the water, making it swirl as it is pushed back. Both sides of the paddle make little bubbles as it is dipped. The canoe is pushed forward after each stroke. The paddles and the canoe leave a path of bubbles behind us. The bubbles leave a trail that fades away slowly as we glide along the water. There is still some ice along both shorelines of the small river.

Moving up the small river, we scare various ducks from the brush. Dad shoots them with the shotgun. There are some ducks that approach us, and Dad shoots them down too. One moment they are flying with precision, and then they fold and crumble as they get hit by the shotgun's pellets. I say it was the ice that kills them as they fall from the sky and land on the hard ice. The ducks are plucked, cleaned, gutted, and washed before we cook them. They make a great meal. The kinds of ducks we hunted and ate were: a-nih-nih-shib (mallard); mah-kah-tay-shib (black mallard), which are now extinct because the smaller mallard has taken over their habitat; pah-kah-koh-shib (the goldeneye) – this duck makes a whistling sound from its wings; and the ahn-zig (merganser). Sometimes Dad hunts ni-ka (goose) and these are very tasty.

Spring trapping is a great time for First Nations here on Mish-kee-ayns Minis (Turtle Island). Spring is called min-noh-gah-mee, meaning "soft earth as the ground melts." The earth comes alive at this time. Everyone wanted to be out on the land at this time of the year.

Our Mom told us stories about dreadful meetings on the reserves just before spring. The meetings had to do with the Hudson's Bay Company store manager and his store clerk. The spring breakup is very treacherous, even for the seasoned trappers and their families. The people had to decide who will stay in the community to look after the clerk and manager and who will leave for spring trapping. Some would say, "But I did it last year!" All First Nations communities in Canada had these Shaa-gun-naa-shee-shug (people who don't tell the truth). There would be discussions for a long time to decide who was going to stay and keep the Hudson's Bay Company men safe on the land and river. The two men were not trained to live outdoors and did not have the knowledge to survive off the land. In previous years, some got lost in the wilderness, some drowned in the river, some fell sick, and some starved to death. If this happened in any community, it looked bad on them. The Hudson's Bay Company did not want to lose any of their personnel. The community members also did not want to have death come to these poor men. But it was a great sacrifice to stay behind. Food, firewood, and friendly company had to be provided for the two men. They were cared for like children.

The journey up the small river takes about a day and we made camp. This camp is only for one night. The next morning is cold and we head down the river. Along the way we pick up all the traps and snares that were set earlier. Most of the traps have muskrats and beavers in them.

Gliding down the river we hear the sounds of spring. The birds that migrated south slowly come back. We hear the moh-noh-gun-nay (flicker), a brown and white woodpecker, make its distinct cry. It starts pounding its rhythmic sound on the dry, dead trees, looking for food. The bih-nay (partridge) can be heard also. Male bih-nay usually find a dead log lying on the ground and sit on it. They puff out their chest and slowly start pounding it with a loud steady beat. The sound suddenly stops after the frantic beating to tell the females that he is the best mate for them. He starts up again as the impulse comes to get the attention that he thinks he deserves. This is the best time to sneak up on them. The bih-nay gets blasted from a shotgun. It makes a good meal.

There is also other partridge we call aakaas-kohg (spruce hens). This partridge is easy to kill. When you shoot one of them, the other ones will come out of the brush to see what you are shooting at. You shoot them too. They never learn.

Kih-chi-kaan-nay-sheenshug (chickadees) stay up in the north all winter. These crazy, busy little birds are always looking for food. When you see a bunch of them together with other birds feeding in a hurry, it tells the people that a storm is coming. In winter they are usually around singing their kih-chi-gee-dee songs. In the spring the males sing a different tune. It goes something like "twee-ee-eet, twee-ee-eet," making it sound like he is saying, "I am here. I am here." The kih-chi-kaan-nay-sheenshug is looking for a mate.

Another bird we looked forward to seeing was the pih-kih-chi (robin). I killed one with my slingshot once and I showed it to Dad. He said it was bad to kill one as they are special birds. I never killed one after that. I remember this because he did not say that about any other birds, especially the aakaas-kohg.

Kah-yaash-koog (seagulls) return with their mournful cries for more food. They fly around and glide in the air, looking for food. They land on their gathering rock that is covered with white streaks of their making. But they did not seem to mind.

We float down the river, picking up the traps and snares. The beavers and the muskrats are put on stretchers to dry out. The dogs are happy when we come back. The tent is put back up along with the stove and its pipes. The tent becomes warm in a short while. The tea kettle is placed on the stove. We are home again.

Another animal that is trapped is the waa-bih-saysh (marten). The waa-bih-saysh has a white patch on his chest. This is why we call it waa-bih-shaysh or "white patch." It is a fur-bearing animal that is bigger than the zhaang-gwaysh (mink). Zhaang-gwaysh also means "a quarter" in Ojibway as mink fur was only worth that much at the time. Its name stuck. That said, it is smaller than the waa-gosh (fox). The marten has a black and brown coat with a tinge of yellow and orange colourings. The marten is a great hunter and it is one of our clans. It is thought of as a great warrior. The marten hunts for smaller animals and it roams over its territory. The traps are set with bait whenever there are tracks appearing in the snow.

We stay in the main camp for about a week. The animal hides are drying out on the stretchers. When the hides are fully dried and put into bags, and when we see the birds come back from the south, this signals that the spring trapping is coming to an end. We prepare to travel down the river to the reserve, Ogoki Post. We break camp. The spring camp is taken down. All of our possessions are put in the canoe. We leave the ten-gallon gas drum, the woodstove, the pipes, dog harness, and traps. These are placed on the tay-saa-kway-guning (wooden platform). They will be used again in the following winter. The sleigh is placed against a tree.

Dad puts the motor on the stern of the canoe. The gas tank is close by. He has a paddle with a long pole we call kaan-da-gee-win-naak. This means "a stick that will propel you forward." He also has the guns nearby. In the middle of the canoe there are pack sacks full of our clothes and blankets. My younger brother and I use these as seats. The animal pelts are in bags and they are in the middle with us. Mom sits at the front of the canoe. Before we leave, she is always taking her time to come down to the canoe as we wait, ready to go. We complain to no avail. She finally comes down and pushes the canoe out. She jumps in the canoe and we are set to go.

The canoe is pushed out and the current points it down towards the reserve. Dad starts up the motor. The canoe is heavy in the water. The water is still cold, running high and very fast. The dogs are untied and want to leap into the canoe while we are still on shore. There is no room for them, so they have to run along the shore alongside us. They look at us before leaving to find out where we are heading down the river. They follow us. During our travel we see them every once in a while. They appear from the woods whenever there is a beach to run along the shore. Sometimes we don't see them for long time. The next time we will see them is when we stop for lunch somewhere down the river.

CHAPTER 12

Geen-na-wind kih-bih-gee-way-min
(We return home)

We have names in the Anishinaabay language for certain areas on the Albany River. There is a place called Kin-noh-shay O-cheet-teeng, meaning "sturgeon's bum." The last waterfall on the river is called Way-coh-chi-wun-naang meaning "the last falls in a se-ries." We also have a waterfall called Saa-geeng Pah-wih-tik, meaning "the rapids where the river comes out from the lake." Ish-pah-quoh-wih-nih-gah-meeng means "where there is a portage with high trees." Shoosh-kwaa-bih-kaa-wih-nih-gahm means "smooth rock falls." Miskoh-bee-gwin-wih-nih-gahm means the "red willow portage." There are the falls called I-kway-wih-nih-gahm, meaning "woman's falls." Keesh-kaa-bih-kaa-wih-nih-gahm means "the falls with sharp pointed rocks that are broken." One of the biggest falls is called Kay-kay-aa-mee, meaning "a place where the fish spawn and can't go further up the river due to the huge falls."

We portage the falls with names that end with the syllables "wih-nih-gahm," as these falls are impossible to shoot with the canoe. There are portages where we unload everything from the canoe. Everything is placed on the ground. The motor is taken off the canoe. Dad turns over the canoe and hoists it up to his shoul-ders. There is a middle strut in the canoe where he can rest the canoe on his shoulders. The stern of the canoe touches the ground. Mom hands Dad two paddles and these are placed on his shoulders. The paddles touch the middle strut and the front strut. Dad bends his knees and balances the canoe as he stands up. The canoe is carried over the portage in this way. Mom, Jerry, and I follow Dad with our belongings that we can carry. At the end of the portage Dad puts down the canoe with the stern part first and holds the canoe up. Dad takes the main cross beam and he slips the canoe off his shoulders slowly and gently puts it down on the ground. We follow behind him like little partridge, carrying our slingshots to bring down any ween-dih-goog (evil spirits).

We return to the items to bring them back to the canoe. Dad puts on a pack sack that has shoulder straps. He puts the twenty-five–pound flour sack on top of that and then he places the motor on top of the flour. His free hand carries the gas tank and the other hand balances the motor. We children carry the smaller items. We get back to the canoe and we stay with Mom while Dad returns to the items again to get the bundles of fur. He puts a thump line across his forehead and the food box is carried on his back. He puts the fur bundles, blankets, and clothes on top of the food box and he carries the guns in both hands. Dad finally returns with the last load and we put everything in the canoe. We push off. The dogs eventually catch up with us. They sense where we are headed.

Some rapids are not severe, and we go over them with every-thing in the canoe. There are other rapids where Mom, Jerry, and I are put on the land and we walk over the portage. Dad takes the canoe with everything in it and he shoots the rapids by himself. Going down the river with all our belongings in the canoe is fun, but we have to stop for a meal. At this point we are about halfway to the reserve. The canoe is pulled up on the shore for lunch. An open fire is made on the shore. The mee-jih-moh-wush (the food box) is taken out of the canoe. The tea kettle is filled with water from the river and placed on the fire. Once again, the dogs catch up with us. They eat and have a rest with us. We eat the choo-chup, the oat mixture with tea. We also have a chunk of cooked beaver leg or a piece of moose meat with the choo-chup. We finish up our lunch, put everything away, put out the fire, and go back in the canoe.

Mom is at the front of the canoe. We push off from the shore. Dad is at the back pulling on the motor and it starts pushing us down the river. The dogs get up and follow us along the shore. They keep up with us for a while and they appear smaller as we go further down the river. We stop just before the reserve to pick them up. They are exhausted. The mean dog, Hoss, is seated with Dad at the back of the canoe. My favourite dog, August, sits in the middle with me. Chop Chop is Jerry's dog, so he sits with him. Chuck, the smart one, sits with Mom in the front of the canoe. The other dogs on the reserve warn the people there that we are approaching. We avoid dog fights by putting our dogs in the canoe.

We move past the old cemetery just before the reserve. At this time, the houses are built all along the northern shore of the Albany River. Each house has a canoe tied up to a dock or pulled up on the shore with a motor tilted to the side. There is a path going up the embankment leading up to the houses. This path is worn down by the people as they walk down to the river to get their drinking water. The river is our drinking water.

We go past these houses until we get to our grandparents' house. It is situated near the end of the reserve. There is an island in front of the house. A little further up the river from here is another island where the Hudson's Bay Company store is located, on the southern side of the Albany River. The store is white and has a red roof. There is also a white picket fence around it. The small Anglican Church is further down the shore from the store. The Catholic Church is on our side of the river. It is the only two-storey building on the reserve. It is further up the river from our grandparents' place. There is a foot path in front of the houses, used by the people to go from the bottom of the reserve to the top. It holds our memories.

We stay at our grandparents' house for about a week. Our Dad takes the fur across the river to sell to the Hudson's Bay Company clerk. He pays off his credit from the previous trip and buys more supplies for our return trip on credit. This happens before the end of June because our brother and sisters have not returned from the residential school yet.

Soon we go back up the river again to Pah-tih-goh-seeng, our spring trapping camp, before continuing up the river to a lake called Kaa-waa-koh-naa-bih-gaag, which means "there are a lot of fish eggs." In the English language, this place is called Caviar Lake. We might stop here or at Monz-zay-wah-geeng (the place where there is moose) or at Washi Lake. These lakes have tourist camps on them where our Dad and uncle will guide the Americans from. They are notified ahead of time where they need to be to meet the tourists. From these lakes they will take the fishermen up or down the river to catch the big one. The prized catch is the speckled trout, the manz-zha-may-goz (the fish that is made in an evil way).

Our parents do commercial fishing at this time of the year. Our uncle and grandparents do the same thing. My brother Jerry and I observe the whole activity while we wait for our older brother and sisters to return from the residential school. Our cousins will also be returning. We know it's about time as it is near the end of June, O-day-min-geesis, the month of strawberries.

On the day of their return, we first hear the sound of the bush plane, the Otter, from a distance somewhere down south. The plane appears and we see it come over the southern shore. It flies over us and we hear the motor make the turn to circle the lake where it is going to land. The plane with its pontoons soars over the lake and we hear it change its sound to slow down. The plane floats over the water a few feet before it touches its surface. The plane moves for a while, cutting the water in two halves, and the pilot slows down the engine. We can see our brother and sisters looking through the windows.

Our Dad and uncle are not here for their return. They are somewhere on the river with the Americans. They will return in the late afternoon. The school kids bring back many new things. There are new clothes, toys, and comic books, and new 45s that have a guy named Elvis singing on them. Their hair is styled in new ways and they speak a little differently. Change has arrived on the Albany River.

We play hide-and-go-seek. I get caught and then have to count from one to ten. I couldn't count to ten in English, so Dad counts for me.

That night I spoke to Dad and said I wanted to go to residential school.

Mom and Dad ask, "Why?"

I said that I want to count from one to ten in English by myself without Dad helping me. Thinking of it now, I might be the only Anishinaabay person that wanted to go to residential school. I was strange. Anishinaabaymowin, the Anishinaabay language, was the only language I understood and spoke at this time. I was five years old. I had to wait for two more years to go.

CHAPTER 13

Nee-bin
(Summer)

School was out for the summer and our older brother and sisters returned home. The residential school is in Lac Seul, just outside of Sioux Lookout. One day our sister Wanda was babysitting us in the tent. She was reading us a bible story about Jesus. This was the beginning of her religious period. She read a page aloud in English and then translated it into Ojibway for us. I started crying at the part where Jesus was crucified. I was so upset that I ran away from the tent and into the bush. Wanda had to get my brothers Angus and Jerry to run after me. Eventually she caught up to me and asked me what was wrong.

I asked, "Why did they kill him?"

That was the end of her bible reading.

Once, back in Ogoki Post, we were in the Anglican Church during church service. I first heard it. I heard the buzz of the mih-zih-zaak (horse fly). The congregation had just filed in. Our grandparents were also there. The first part of the service was the singing of the selected hymn. Our grandfather would belt out the song in the loudest voice. Everyone hated his singing! He couldn't carry a tune. But he didn't seem to notice. The songs were all in Ojibway. After the singing, I saw the mih-zih-zaak again. It was flying up high in the ceiling trying to get out. Or it might be trying to escape from Choo-mis's (grandfather's) singing.

The mih-zih-zaak in church landed on one of the upper rafters. It flew off to the corner in the ceiling and it got caught in a spider's web. The mih-zih-zaak knew it was in big trouble. It tried to get loose from the web, but the harder it tried the more tangled it got. The vibrations in the web alerted the a-sub-bih-kay-cheens (web maker). From the shadows, it scurries out onto the web and stops to check its prey. When it saw the spider there was a moment of stillness from the mih-zih-zaak. Then it went into a frenzy of movement to get away. The a-sub-bih-kay-cheens crept in slowly to inspect its catch. It crept closer still to the mih-zih-zaak before pouncing on it. The mih-zih-zaak struggled and struggled as its life was sucked out. It seemed to shrink in size. Then it stopped moving. While this was going on our grandfather started to sing again.

We feared the mih-zih-zaak whenever we went swimming. They seem to know where to land on you so that you won't be able to hit them. They take chunks of your flesh out and lap up the pooling blood. Their relative, the mih-zih-zaa-koons (deer fly), is even worse. They are smaller but their bite is even worse. They buzz around your head, but it is hard to swipe them away. If you had curly hair, they got caught in it. It was only then that you could squish them dead.

Our little Anishinaabay congregation had travelled across the river to meet in church. All the canoes were pulled up on the steep embankment. The various motors were tilted at different angles. After church we went to the Hudson's Bay Company store to buy candy and pop. I had Orange Crush. We returned to our homes a little bit holy. The church thing was not for us as we had to leave to go up the river again. The summers go fast. In late August, somewhere along the Albany River, students wait for the sound of the plane.

When our siblings went back to school, we travelled up the river much faster. It is getting colder. We will not return to Ogoki Post as we have bought all of our winter supplies. We ended up on one of the lakes where the American tourists would come to fish or hunt. We always set our nets to catch fish to eat and also to feed the dogs. Our ancestors always fished using the net. They saw the a-sub-bih-kay-cheens make one and learned from him. The net is always placed in special areas that were owned by certain families. No one else was allowed to come into our traditional hunting territory, and we were not allowed to hunt and fish in other people's areas.

Mom, Dad, Jerry, and I sit in the middle of the canoe as we approach the powerful Kay-kay-a-mee (the falls where the fish can't go up). We are forced to portage. As Dad turns off the motor to glide the canoe into the landing, Mom tells us a story of the water serpent. She points to a rock sticking out of the water near the bottom of the falls. The white, foamy water circles around the back of the rock as it stood its ground against the power of the falls. It sends the bubbles away down the river. Mom says that our grandparents once made this trip on their own when they were younger. At this very spot they saw a huge, green, slimy water serpent come out of the water behind the rock. It had tiny arms with sharp claws. It looked down one side of the rock and then the other. It then dove into the water to catch something to eat. The story came from Choo-mis (grandfather) and Kokum (grandmother) so it must be true.

We were scared before the canoe hit the shore. We stuck closely to our parents throughout the portage. We secretly looked back at the rock as we went up the portage, holding onto our slingshots tightly.

Jerry and I asked to carry one of the guns but were refused. Mom and Dad said that we might accidentally shoot ourselves.

"How about the paddle, then?" we ask.

"No," says Mom, "it is being used by Dad now."

"How about the axe?"

"No," she says, "you might cut yourself."

"How about the buck saw?"

"No, you might lose it."

We stuck close to our parents after the portage at Kay-kay-a-mee.

Later I learned that these stories were meant to scare us so that we listened to our parents and elders. It is a form of discipline to keep us in line. They worked. We did not go down to the edge of the falls to play and delay our journey up the river. It also prevented us from falling into the water and drowning. We were also very mindful of the water serpents when we went swimming. We never swam alone or swam at night. We were zay-gis; we were afraid.

One of my first introductions to the outside world was when the Americans came to hunt and fish on our lands during the summer and in the fall. Our mom didn't like the American hunters and fishermen that treated her with kindness. She would carry pails of drinking water from the river and one of the Americans would say, "Oh, Mrs Baxter, please let me carry that for you." She knew that she was not a helpless woman. She could survive in the wilderness for a very long time all by herself. The Americans did not know this about Anishinaabay I-kway-wug (women), that they were all taught how to live in the wilderness. She always resented the fact they thought she was helpless, but they were also just showing kindness. She liked the majority of them. The Americans that Dad guided always came to our camp for a visit after their day of fishing. They would sit by the fire and tell us their stories, which I never understood at the time. They seemed to enjoy them.

One of the stories Mom and Dad told us later, as we were getting older, was the time that one of the American fishermen came over for a visit during their stay. Our grandparents had their tent near our camp site and the American fisherman really liked our Choo-mis (grandfather). Our Dad had just finished making supper and Choo-mis was standing nearby when the fisherman approached them. He was a bit tipsy from drinking.

He saw Choo-mis and called out to him, saying, "Hey, George, you ole' son of a bitch! How are you?"

Our grandfather answered with, "A-nay ay-i-kit-tooch? Asubka-inabich nay i-kit-toh?" (What is he saying? The way the net is set, is this what he is saying?).

We still get a chuckle over that.

Ki-chi Mo-koh-man-a-keeng means "the land of the big knives" and also refers to the United States. Our Dad and uncles guided American fishermen and moose hunters from all over Ki-chi Mo-koh-man-a-keeng. They came from cities such as Detroit, Michigan; Little Rock, Arkansas; Des Moines, Iowa; Chicago, Illinois; Milwaukee, Wisconsin, and many others. Mom created beaded moccasins for the families of some of the Americans. They also ordered moose hide mitts and a few wanted special moose hide jackets. All of the jackets were made with beads and had fringes on them. The orders would be taken one year, and when the hunters and fishermen returned the following year, the items were sold. The American tourists were big tippers; well, some of them.

The traditional fishing season started 20 May and ended on 15 September. The hunting season started on that same day, 15 September. The Americans brought their high-powered rifles with them. These rifles were equipped with very powerful scopes that could pick off an ant at a hundred yards. These weapons were used to bring down big moose with big racks. We were often scared for the moose. Dad and our uncles only had .30-30 rifles with no scope, which are not terribly powerful. Instead of a powerful scope, they simply used an open sight. They were true hunters. They did not need every advantage.

Dad told us that guiding the American moose hunters was dangerous. The guides made sure the guns were not loaded when they came in and out of the canoe. They always told the hunters to check if there were any live bullets in the chamber.

Once there was a hunter that came into camp with an elephant gun. He loved that gun. The hunter was sitting up at the front of the canoe while his hunting partner sat in the middle. The hunter in the front of the canoe was loading his elephant gun when the gun went off. There was a loud explosion and a big spray of water. The water came gushing into the canoe. The hunter scrambled quickly to get in the middle of the canoe with his prized gun. Dad sped up the motor so that the front end of the canoe rose above the water line. They returned to the shore. The hunter was so scared. He gave Dad money to be quiet about it so that the hunter didn't get in trouble with the tourist operator. Dad pulled the canoe on the shore and turned it over. The hole was fixed using ambroid glue and a large patch of canvas. Before ambroid glue, birch bark or canvas canoes would be patched with spruce gum. The hunters and Dad waited a while for the glue to harden and away they went.

The moose hunters were guided to certain areas where the moose gathered. This time of the year was mating season. In order to entice the male moose out of the bush you had to make the sounds of a female. The female moose has a soft call, sounding like "aawh." The male moose would hear this sound and charge out of the bush, thrashing its huge antlers. This act of aggression was to show the females how powerful he was and that he had beat the other male moose in a duel. This was the one that got shot.

Dad told us that he and the American hunters with their expensive guns would come upon a huge moose with big antlers standing broadside in the bush. The hunters would empty their guns on the moose, and it would slowly turn around and walk away. The hunters would quickly reload their expensive guns and start firing again, this time even more wildly. During the shooting Dad takes his .30-30 rifle with the open sight and shoots the moose dead. The hunters are happy, and Dad is happy. He did not lose a big tip.

One summer we went to town at the end of June. This is the time when my brother and sisters returned from residential school. We lived in a tent down by the airplane base. There is a small town there called Nakina. The town was a few miles away from the base. We left our dogs at home with our uncle. Dad gave me a puppy around that time. I called it Mahovlich after the hockey player Frank Mahovlich. Our dad went to Nakina with a load of our belongings first and he took the puppy with him. By the time Mom, Jerry, and I arrived in Nakina the puppy had died; it was sitting on the road with the other town dogs when a car came along. All the other dogs moved off the road but for Mahovlich.

Gii-sis Pih-ah-goh-chin (The sun is rising).
The new day represents the changes that happened
to the Anishinaabayg during residential school.

PART THREE

Residential school

Nihtahwemahgunug kii-izhaawug kahisihtaanihwung
kahkihnohmaagewin.
(My siblings went to the residential school.)
Niibing giipihgiiwewug.
(In the summer they came home.)
Kiitahshaagunaashiimohwug.
(They really could speak English.)
Odahminohyaang kaasohwin aiitush andohwaabungihgen
niinduhm cih agindaasohyaan kawiin ningiikihkendahziin
cih agindaasohyaan pezhig aiitush midaaswi abahcihtooyaan
Shaagunaashiimowin.
(When we played hide-and-seek and it was my turn to count,
I did not know how to count from one to ten in English.)
Nidedem giiagindaasoh.
(My dad counted.)
Kahdihbihkung ningiiwiintahmohwaag nihdede, nihmaamaa
keniinnihwii-izha kahkihnohmaagewining.
(That evening I told my Dad and Mom that I also wanted
to go to school.)

Ningii-izhaa Pelican Kahisihtaanihwung Kahkihnohmaagewin
    wetih Sioux Lookout, Ontario.
(I went to the Pelican Residential School in Sioux Lookout,
    Ontario.)
Aiitushke Shingwauk Kahisihtaanihwung Kahkihnohmaagewin
    wetih Pahwihtigong.
(And also to Shingwauk Residential School in Sault Ste Marie,
    Ontario.)
Ningiishaabohkaanun.
(I survived them.)

CHAPTER 14

Mee-na-waa giga-waabamin
(I'll see you again)

"Ni-wee-i-zha kay-neen!"

"(I want to go, too!)"

This was my request and desire to go to school. It came from the fact that I couldn't count from one to ten in English. My older brother and sisters came back every summer from residential school. Our older cousins also could count to ten because they knew English. Every time they came back, we played hide-and-seek. I would get caught and I had to count from one to ten. I could not count from one to ten in English. Our Dad had to count for me. I didn't like that. That evening I told my Mom and Dad that I wanted to go to school. I was probably the only Anishinaabay that wanted to go to residential school, so they could count from one to ten in English.

We were picked up by a bush plane.

At the end of every August, one of the planes with pontoons landed on the water to get us. These were usually a de Havilland Beaver, a Norseman, or a Twin Beechcraft. My older brother, my three sisters, and my cousins were all stuffed into the planes. We flew from Washi Lake and landed in Nakina. Nakina was a small railway town. They would feed us in a restaurant there. The woman that worked there had a crooked neck. We called her "pee-mih-koh-yaaow" (crooked neck). The Nakina Hotel was the only place in town that could accommodate us. We slept there for the night. We awoke the next morning and waited for the Canadian National Railway train that would take us west to the town of Sioux Lookout. There were quite a number of us Anishinaabayg waiting for the trains – there were other kids from isolated reserves including Eabametoong (Fort Hope), Nibinamik (Summer Beaver), Webequie (the head moving sideways), and Neskantaga (Landsdowne House).

We arrived at the train station in Sioux Lookout and were put on a bus that took us to Pelican Lake Indian Residential School. This was the last time we would be together as a family. The school officials first separated us into boys and girls, and then split each group into three parts. There were the juniors, the intermediates, and the seniors. It was like Hogwarts in the Harry Potter books.

The school was huge. One side of the top floor housed the junior boys and the other side housed the junior girls. The floor below housed the intermediate boys with the intermediate girls on the other side. Under this floor were the senior boys and girls, separated of course. The lower floor held the principal's office, the two recreation rooms, and, of course, the chapel. Many of the school supervisors also lived on the lower floor.

In several residential schools in Canada, the ages were as follows: junior boys and girls four to eight years old, intermediate boys and girls nine to twelve years old, and senior boys and girls thirteen to sixteen years old. There was no education program for us after the age of sixteen. There was the opportunity to attend college and university, but we had to give up our Indian status to do so. The law was changed before I went to university, thankfully.

The Pelican Lake Residential School opened in 1926 and first held 135 students. After World War II, this number increased to around 160. The children who went spoke only Ojibway, Cree, and Swampy Cree. This would soon change. They came from everywhere; collected inside an area of 686,000 square kilometres in Northern Ontario. I was taken there at the age of six years.

On arrival, we were given clothes, shoes, and lockers. We were given numbers to our lockers, too. This number was also put on our clothes.

We were separated from our sisters and older brothers. We were not allowed to speak in Ojibway ever. Since I only spoke Ojibway, communication became very difficult. This is where our hunting sense came into being. We used our listening skills that we developed in the bush so that we became quiet. We also watched our surroundings carefully. The Ojibway language was spoken to us only to explain something. It was also used by people that you trusted absolutely. What was expected from the supervisors came through to us by watching what the other students were doing. We missed our parents.

I remember our Dad came on the train to residential school with us once. The train was going around the bend and we saw the lead car. Dad made a comment that the lead car was Chuck, the head dog for our dog team. I don't know what happened to Dad when we reached Sioux Lookout. I guess he went back to Nakina with Chuck.

The junior boys' dormitory was huge and held single beds. There was a big bathroom that had round sinks to wash our hands. We had to push on a round bar with our feet to get the water flowing. This was also where we brushed our teeth. Every Saturday we had to wash the floors in the bathroom and in the dormitory. The toilets had to be washed as well. The hallway and the stairs had to be swept and washed. These were our chores. We got to play outside in the afternoon.

We settled in our dormitories with all of us brushing our teeth, putting on our pyjamas, and kneeling by our beds with our hands together to pray. There were many routines we had to follow. Lining up in rows was a big thing. We lined up for everything. One time for supper we were in the boys' gym lining up when I saw one of my sisters on the girls' side. I broke away from the line and ran across the dining room calling her name. The boys' supervisor grabbed me from behind and yanked me back into line.

At night we were given clean pyjamas, toothbrushes, and a chance to go the bathroom. We had our own little beds. Everyone had to kneel beside their bed. Our hands were placed together in prayer. We closed our eyes to pray in English. We didn't know the language of the Lord, so we did not know who we were praying to. Then the lights were turned off. The crying started.

Our beds had to be made precisely, with the sheets tucked in using the "nurse tuck." The bed cover had to be tight enough so that a coin could bounce on it. At the end of the bed was a small blanket that was called the fire blanket. It was used for extra warmth and for fire drills. We had fire drills that terrified the junior boys. At night, the supervisor woke us to line up in front of a black hole. This was actually a small door that opened into round metal tubes that ran all the way down to the bottom of the school. It was terrifying to enter the black hole in the middle of the night with the wind whistling outside. The fire blanket was placed at the entrance of the door and we would struggle and fight not to get on it. They threw us on the blanket anyway and pushed us down the dark tube. We flew down the tube on these magic carpets and landed hard on the ground. Some of us bounced on the ground a couple of times. The older boys were at the bottom of the tube to catch us, but it seems us unfavourable junior boys were allowed to slide by and hit the ground. We did not like fire drills.

We all had the same haircuts. The boys were shaved down to the skull. The girls were given short, straight bob cuts. The idea behind these cuts were to get rid of any lice. I have heard stories where students were doused on the scalp with kerosene. The scalp sizzled as soon as the kerosene hit the skin.

There we all stood around with our short haircuts and our ears sticking out all over the place. The boys with ears that severely stuck out were teased mercilessly. They were called "mah-mung-gih-ta-wug," meaning "big ears." I was one of these boys. That hurt.

The three groups of boys were made to line up for breakfast, lunch, and supper. The boys and girls lined up with the juniors first, then the intermediates, and then the seniors. We lined up on our side of the building to enter the dining room. We both entered the dining room from our respective playrooms. The girls went to their side of the dining room and we went to our side. We were not allowed to sit with our sisters. We were not people, we were numbers.

During the first year of residential school, we watched what the other students were doing and followed their example. We learned what was expected from us. We were not allowed to speak in the language we already knew. There were only certain safe times to speak. We talked to our relatives in secret places, like in the wilderness during the weekend.

We were the junior boys. None of us knew how to speak English. We knew instinctively not to use the Ojibway language in any way. But being told not to do something, we did it anyway. No self-respecting Ojibway listened to authority. We talked in the language when no supervisor was around. The older boys were given incentives like candy when they reported the younger boys using the language. They would tell on us even if we did not speak in the language. We were placed at the highest level in the building, but we were treated the lowest. The intermediate and senior boys pushed us around. They took our food. We would receive candy from the canteen every Saturday, but we would have to give it to the older boys waiting outside or else. They ate while we cried.

A junior boy is picked on by an intermediate boy. The junior boy tells his older brother, a senior boy, and the intermediate boy is beaten up. The intermediate boy's older brother then gets involved. There is a fight amongst the senior boys. There was this cycle of violence in the school. A boy or girl who did not have an older brother or sister was picked on relentlessly.

Once the older boys went into town for a doctor checkup. The boys were told to strip down to their underwear. It was very difficult for them to take off their clothes in the doctor's office as there was a young nurse in the room with them. When the doctor told this one boy to take his underwear down, something else went up. To remedy the situation, the doctor slapped down the problem with his stethoscope.

Every Saturday night we watched Western films. They were in black and white, on reel-to-reel. Randolph Scott carried two guns and, while smoking, kept shooting at the charging Indians. He was the good guy. He killed many Indians. He was very good at it. We all aspired to be like him. There was usually a girl in the movie. The good guy always ended up with the girl. The kissing would start, and we didn't like that.

We categorized the Cowboys as the good guys and the Indians as the bad guys. The main character was always the good guy and we called him "kaa-nu-gah-cheech," meaning "the one who had good moves." The Indian was usually portrayed as a savage with a monolithic speech pattern; what we called the "ug" speech. We were always the bad guys.

The older boys gathered us together to play Cowboys and Indians. The older boys were always the Cowboys and the younger boys were always the Indians. Us Treaty 9 boys were always the Indians, as we were on Treaty 4 territory. We were killed even though we shot the others dead first. They said they moved at the last minute so that we missed them. We never won. One of my older cousins was captured once by the good guys. He was tied to a tree and left outside. The older boys told us not to tell the boys' supervisor where he was. The time came for us to come inside for supper. We were asked where he was. We couldn't tell so the supervisor believed that there was a "runner." My cousin spent the night outside in the cold. The next morning someone told the supervisor where he was.

The CBC's *Hockey Night in Canada* was always watched in the recreation room. There were only boys there at this time. We were given peanut butter sandwiches with jam on thick white bread. This was a treat for us. We had very good hockey players in the intermediate and senior boys. Everybody was into hockey. I was only interested in sandwiches.

On Sunday nights we watched *Bonanza*. When the music came on, Pa Cartwright and his sons rode up and they were introduced: Ben, Little Joe, Hoss, Adam. The Chinese character, Hop Sing, was introduced later. A map of Ponderosa appeared on screen and then it quickly burned away. You never saw any women introduced. We were given ice cream. It was very good, but it gave us terrible gas.

Dick and Jane were other characters that I had problems with. The reading series had Spot and Fluffy as their pets. They lived in a nice house with a white picket fence. I couldn't relate to their lifestyle. The only white picket fences I knew were the ones used for graves. I didn't understand what they were about. I still couldn't read. I repeated kindergarten.

It is known by us survivors and by the Department of Indian Affairs that many native kids were put in provincial and federal jails. Why? The jails were better than residential schools. In jail you received better meals, better television, and a better place to sleep. This was especially the case during the cold winter months. Besides, most of their friends were there for the winter, too.

CHAPTER 15

Queen Elizabeth mah-mung-gih-zit
(Queen Elizabeth big feet)

The school supervisors were strange. One supervisor always wore striped shirts. We called him chaa-chi-gaa-wih-gun, meaning "the one who has stripes." Another supervisor looked after the school's farm. He had a long, pointed nose. The tractor he used made him move around on the seat and bounced his head back and forth so that he looked like a woodpecker. We called him Pah-pah-say (the Woodpecker).

There was this other supervisor that the girls loved. He was young and handsome; he knew it. One time we were eating supper in the dining room. The tables close to the walls were a tight squeeze to pass through and the supervisors were always hovering around. A young female supervisor was going around the back of the girls close to the wall. The young male supervisor ran around to her side and tried to pass behind the female supervisor. This made a loud cheer from the boys and girls alike. He stood closely behind her smiling. She was smiling, too.

The farm that Pah-pah-say oversaw was not a working farm when we were there. All the animals were gone. The farm's entire field was cleared by former students. The principal's house was situated south of the barn. The land did not have any trees. The clearing of the trees happened before our Dad's time.

Our Dad and uncles worked the farm when they attended residential school. There was not much academic work done back then. A story we always ask Dad to tell was when one of our uncles fed the pigs. Our uncle was always angry at school and he took it out on the pigs. He was always kicking at them as the pigs crowded around to feed. There was this one pig that he hated the most. After feeding the pigs one day, our Dad and uncle were standing around talking when our uncle was knocked off his feet by the pig he hated. Our uncle landed on the dirty floor covered with their droppings. The pig got his revenge.

We became homesick. The huge lake in front of the residential school did not help at all. A small river drained into the lake. We played in the woods near there. But the best place to play was along the shoreline. It reminded me of running our boats with the string along the water. It felt like home.

The leaves had changed colours. The days were getting colder. The birds were starting to migrate. I saw the same birds that I saw at home. The birds reminded me of my mother and father, and I wanted to have them come to me. I became pure by acting good to everyone I encountered. I thought I gained enough purity that the birds would come to me. I thought the birds would become my friends. But they didn't want anything to do with me. Maybe it was the wrong time of year. They had other things on their mind. This was the time I thought I could be so pure that birds would visit me.

One day I lost track of time as I was hunting a bird in the wilderness with my slingshot. The quietness outside told me that everyone was inside. When I returned, it was so late that I did not receive any supper that night. I was sent back to the dormitory. It was windy outside with a hard rain. I was watching the storm through the windows of the washroom. Just then I saw the roof of the barn collapse.

All of us were given lockers for our clothes. They gave us Sunday clothes, too. These were a white shirt, a tie, a jacket, black pants, white socks, and black shoes. Our number was written on each of them. Every Sunday morning and evening we had to attend church service. We dressed up in our Sunday best. The chapel in the school was filled with the boys on one side and the girls on the other side. The hymns were sung by us. The preacher delivered his sermon, which none of us juniors could understand. To this end, the youngest students did not understand much of the service. But we did things that we did not understand. We said things that we did not understand.

One winter morning, on a Saturday, a supervisor said he was going hunting. He said that the students who did not have a cold were allowed to join him. That didn't matter. I had a bad cold at the time, but I suppressed my cough. The ground crunched as we walked down the road. A smaller road took us into the woods covered with snow. We were told to be quiet. A white man with a gun trailed by twenty Indian students must have looked funny to an outsider. We saw a partridge; we all turned rigid. The supervisor took aim, and then I coughed. The bird took off into the bush. I was never asked to go hunting again.

I passed kindergarten on my second try. The junior students went to a schoolhouse near the residential school for lessons. We sat at wooden desks that had a writing board in front of us. Under the seat was a drawer where we put our books. One of the routines we did was stand for the national anthem, "O Canada." I would get so nervous doing spelling exercises. The teacher would give us small, individual letters from the English alphabet and ask us to make words with them at our desk. It was like the game Scrabble. The words were then written on the blackboard for everyone in the classroom to see. Getting the letters to stay in the correct order was nerve-racking. A person may have all the letters in a straight line but would sneeze and make a mess of them. It was best to hold your breath.

To make me feel better I took out my frustration on the Queen. Her picture was everywhere. I called her Queen Elizabeth mah-mung-gih-zit, meaning "Queen Elizabeth Big Feet." This was the beginning of my rhyming phase where I used the English language with Ojibway words. I did this for a while until I felt really guilty about it. I asked the teacher to go to the bathroom. On the way to the bathroom, in the hall, there was a picture of Queen Elizabeth. I stood in front of her and asked for her forgiveness. This was one of my moments of pureness; then I went pee. I felt better after that.

The feeling of purity didn't last, however. I returned to my desk. The teacher was giving a lesson and we went to do our work. I sat wondering if anyone noticed my act of pureness. Out of nowhere, a wooden pointer smashed onto my writing area. I jumped up with a start. The teacher shouted at me, asking why I wasn't doing my work. I was so scared. I did my work from then on. My pureness was gained and lost in a single moment.

In the spring I used to walk through the fields looking at the flowers, the dragonflies, the butterflies, and the birds coming back from the south. There were these bright yellow flowers growing along the ditches near the residential school. I gathered some of them and went to the principal's house. I knocked and his wife came to the door. I handed her the flowers. I don't know what she said but she gave me a big red apple. I returned with flowers many times after that.

CHAPTER 16

O-daa-min-noh-taa
(Let's play)

The first-year students arrived with us when I started my second year at residential school. We knew the routines by then. The younger students were told not to use the Ojibway language before they left their communities.

Once in the early fall we went for a long walk down a gravel road. Of course, we had on our new clothes. We came to a bridge and we all looked down into the moving water. One of the new boys had his foot dangling over the side when one of his new shoes came off. We watched as it sailed down to the river below and splashed into the water. The boy could not tell his supervisor about it as he could not speak English, and he knew that he couldn't speak about it in Ojibway. He suffered in silence wearing one shoe for a long time.

I won first prize for academics at the end of grade two. My academic career started that year. I was finally starting to understand English. My reward was a cowboy outfit. It came with two shiny guns with a full holster of bullets. There was also a black cowboy hat and sporty cowboy boots. I wore the outfit that night in the dormitory. I practiced drawing my guns and I had my hat placed in such a way to look mean. That was the only time I got to wear my outfit. They were gone by the next morning, stolen by the other boys. It was the end of my cowboy career.

When the school year ended all of our clothes were placed in paper bags for us to take home. Our Christmas toys were placed in the bags, too; that is, the ones that were not stolen. We boarded the train in Sioux Lookout to go back to Nakina. I remember looking at the communication lines placed along the tracks. They flew past us as we moved closer to Nakina. Some of the poles were on dry, even ground; others were on high ground. Some leaned towards the tracks while others pulled away from them and sat in the middle of a swamp. The wires were pulled straight and some were taut, each alive with electric talk.

I kept in my pocket small, round black marbles. They were smaller than regular marbles and they squeaked when they were squeezed together in my hand. I popped a couple of the marbles into my mouth. The marbles were moving around in circles in my mouth when the train hit a bump in the tracks and I accidentally swallowed them. I began choking. I was scared. A couple of the older boys rushed over to me, bent me over, and pounded my back with their hands. Thankfully the marbles flew out of my mouth when we hit another bump. One of the older boys shouted, "So this is what happened to the Chinese checkers!"

All the boys had black plastic combs sticking out of their back pockets. The combs were our personal possessions. They had a dual purpose. One of the ways we used our combs was to play hockey. The gym had a big concrete floor; this was our ice. The goalie posts were the two shoes from the goalie. The puck was a rolled-up piece of black tape. The comb was the hockey stick. We played on our knees. The combs were curved at the tip to get better shots. We "pahsh-kih-sih-gay-min" (we shot) and we "peen-chi-way-bih-naam-min" (we scored). The games were played before supper and when it was raining outside. These games were intense.

The combs were also used to slick our hair back. The younger boys' hair was always short due to their buzz cuts. We slicked it back with water and this made our hair stick out like porcupines with ears sticking out. We thought we looked cool!

The hair was combed straight back on both sides of the head. At the ears the hair was combed towards the middle of the scalp. The hair came together from both sides and created a small valley. It looked like two black rivers cascading down together. The back part was like that, too. The hair on both sides is combed towards the middle. The hairs meet and are combed down at the back. The duck tail is created by combing the hair out and up. We looked like the rear-end of a mallard duck flying south for the winter.

The intermediate boys did a better job with their longish hair. They tried hard to copy the senior boys. The older boys had longer hair; they had more to work with. The poor boys used water to create the duck tail look at the back of their head. The front part had the "Superman" curl. But water dried fast and made their hairdos fade quickly.

There were other varying products used to keep the style in place. The next best thing to water was Vaseline. It lasted longer and kept hair in place. The best product was by far Brylcreem, but it was expensive so only the boys with money could afford it. The hair froze solid when playing hockey outside. It became something like a helmet. High winds could not move that hair out of place. A bodycheck did not disturb a single thread of hair. A direct hit by a puck to a head full of Brylcreem would dent the puck.

Some of the more desperate boys at school used white lard, the same we would cook with. It was lightly coloured and greasy to the touch. The hair of these boys was shiny, but it did not attract girls, only flies!

We all kept marbles in our pockets, under our pillows, and in our lockers. The game we played with marbles had many aspects to it. The ground was cleared and smoothed out for the marbles to roll towards a hole we dug in the ground. We pushed the marbles toward the hole using our pointer finger. The finger was bent at an angle and the thumb was place at the back of the finger. This resembled the putter used in golf. The players started by pushing their marbles towards the hole. The idea was to try to get the marbles into the hole or close to it. The marbles are spread along the ground. The player with the marble closest to the hole started. He took a marble and placed it on his thumb. The thumb was flicked with the marble and aimed to the opponent's closest marble. We were able to hit the marble and our marble replaced the marble that was moved. The player then pushed his marbles towards the hole. When he missed the hole, the other player started their turn. The game ended when one player pushed all of their marbles into the hole. That player took all of the marbles in the hole. A person asks their brothers or friends for manzih-nay-gay-say (credit) of five marbles to get back into the game. The person is paid back with the five marbles and a couple extra as interest.

The marbles were categorized depending on their markings. A plain marble wasn't worth anything. A marble with fancy swirls was worth three plain marbles. A clear, see-through marble was worth five plain marbles. The most sought-after marble was the steelie. It was basically a ball bearing. It was worth ten marbles. Marbles were our currency.

Being in Lac Seul was hard. We were separated from our sisters. The younger boys and girls were herded away from their older siblings. We lost our protection. We were on our own. It was dangerous. Our Dad came to visit us for Christmas once in Lac Seul. It was so great to see him. We introduced him to our friends; we played games and listened to stories. We got to stay with him in the recreation room. Mom did not make the trip. She knew it would have been too hard on us children emotionally. It would have been too hard for her. Dad didn't visit us at school during the holidays after that. I imagine that he felt too much.

CHAPTER 17

Elvis Kih-chi Zii-bii
(Elvis of Albany River)

The train arrived in Nakina with our luggage and all the happy students flying back to their homes. We were taken down to Twin Lakes, where the float planes were based. A huge blue truck owned by Austin Airways took us there. I remember there was a huge wooden fence around the back of the truck. Once onboard we held onto our luggage and looked out as the dust from the gravel road rose up behind us. We were all excited. We felt light. The float plane took us back to our territory, to our homeland.

When we would return from residential school our parents were either at Washi Lake, Ogoki Post reserve, Kaa-waa-koh-naa-bih-kaag (Caviar Lake), which was a spawning ground, or at Moo-shay-wa-keeng (Grassy Lake), the place where moose are. We would always find our parents through word of mouth. Our language was heard again. Our parents were glad for us to be back, I think.

Back home we did not have electricity. It did not matter if we were sleeping on the ground with just our blankets under the canvas tent. We were with our family again. Nothing else held meaning. We all walked along the shoreline again. Our slingshots were ready to be used against Wendigo and the water serpents again.

The dogs were happy for us to be home again, too. They ran along the shore in the sand and disappeared into the woods. But they always came home.

I know what Cinderella must have felt like. I would get up early in the morning to complete my chores. The water had to be fetched by me. I went down to the river with my two pails and dragged them back to camp. The water would disappear, and I'd have to go to the water again. At this time my younger brother was still too young to get the water. My older brother was now too old to get the water. I was just right. Sometimes I wouldn't finish my chores until late at night.

Elvis came to the shores of Albany River. Our sisters loved Elvis Presley. He was constantly being played on our battery-operated turntable. His picture was on the album covers that my sisters had. Mom, Dad, and our aunts and uncles called him "Elabus." My older brother and male cousins combed their hair just like him. They also tried to sing like him. Imagine hearing "Hound Dog" or "Blue Suede Shoes" with an Anishinaabemowin twang.

We lived in canvas tents during the summer. We cooked most of our food outside. We even ate on the ground outside. Our huge tea kettle was placed in the open fire. The water boils and Mom or Dad throws in the tea bags. The food is served on steel plates. Our dogs sat on the ground with their tails swishing side to side, waiting for scraps. This is the time when we told our stories.

Usually Mom and Dad would go first. Then our brother and sisters would tell theirs. More and more our stories were now in a mix of English and Ojibway. This was a time for great laughter. We laughed to push away the knowledge that we would be leaving again for school. We huddled by the fire more and more frequently, telling our stories. The smoke got into our eyes. Our older sister Ruth said that we would arrive at school with red eyes due to the smoke. "Ka-miskoh-bih-chaa-bih-min," she would say. But our red eyes came from somewhere else.

In a blink we would be back at the train station. In another we would be back in our beds at residential school, the place where the crying began.

Our Dad ordered our back-to-school clothes from the Eaton's or Sears catalogues in July. Thankfully he included us in the process. He probably knew the hell we'd pay at school if we looked out of place. After the ordering was done, we used the catalogue paper as toilet paper. It was not soft.

I remember the time that I wanted Dad to order me a blue suitcase. I wanted to go back to school in style, so to speak. The old potato sacks we used for suitcases were not for me anymore. I was growing older and more conscious of my appearance. My Dad said no. I cried and stamped my feet, but it did not work. My blue suitcase did not arrive when our orders came in from the catalogue. I arrived at school with a canvas potato sack for a suitcase. Our Dad was smart. He knew that no one was going to steal a potato sack.

One year we turned left at Nakina instead of right to Sioux Lookout. No one told me that we were not returning to Pelican Lake. Instead, the train headed towards Shingwauk Residential School in Sault Ste Marie, Ontario. It wasn't until years later that I found out why we were sent there.

One of our cousins, Charlie, came home one summer from Pelican Lake with a black eye. He had a fight with one of the boys from Treaty 4 territory. They did not like us as we were from Treaty 9. My uncle complained to the agent for the Department of Indian Affairs. Our uncle said the Baxter kids were not going back to the Pelican school. The Indian agent finally agreed, and we were sent to Shingwauk. The Crees, who we called Mush-kee-goog (marsh people), were already there. So rather than fight with Treaty 4 kids, we fought them instead. The Mush-kee-goog said it was their school because they were there first.

This is how school started for us in Shingwauk.

CHAPTER 18

Nin-gee shoosh-kwa-tay-min
(We skated)

We boarded the train in Nakina and went to Hornepayne, a small train station in Algoma District. We changed trains. The Algoma Central Railway took us to Sault Ste Marie. Shingwauk Indian Residential School was situated near St Mary's River. It was on a huge property. The main building was very large.

Shingwauk was originally built in 1873 in Garden River First Nation and was operated by the Anglican Church. Six days after its opening, the school was destroyed by fire. A new school was built in 1875 in Sault Ste Marie on ninety acres of land. It had no running water or electricity, and fifty students. Years later, in 1935, the Church and government built a new school to hold around 140 students. On a farm next to the school is a cemetery. The land was donated by a local farmer. In it lies the remains of more than 120 former students. Only school administrators got headstones. We got cheap wooden crosses that were stolen or rotted away.

We got off the bus in front of the building. There were these huge concrete stairs leading into the building. Inside, we came to the principal's office. Straight ahead was a hall leading to the chapel. Nearby the principal's office was a long hall; the left led to the boys' side and the right led to the girls' side. The junior boys and girls were housed on the top floor, the intermediates had the next floor, and the seniors had the lower floor. In the basement were the playrooms and they were separated by a huge dining room. It was basically the same setup as Pelican, since the same design for residential school buildings was used across Canada. The main entrances for the boys and girls were at the back of the building. After that first day, we never used the front entrance again.

Unlike Pelican Lake, this school did not have the tube fire escapes. Instead it had black steel staircases with landings. They were more user-friendly during fire escape drills. You could go down them at your own speed. They were also quieter when you escaped at night. At Pelican, the students attempting escape through the tube were overheard by everyone as they tumbled down to freedom.

Shingwauk was below Bah-wih-tig (The Falls), and we walked to the river every chance we got. It reminded us of home, of the Albany River. We used to walk across Queen Street to get to there. Close to this road was the main chapel. We heard stories that a student was killed inside the chapel and his ghost appeared every once in a while.

There were two more chapels inside the main building at Shingwauk: a little one and a big one. We had Sunday services at night in the bigger chapel. The smaller chapel was to the left of the principal's office and across the hall. It also had a piano in it. One night there was a commotion down by the little chapel. The senior boys and their supervisor heard the piano being played loudly. Everybody was in bed by then. They went to the small chapel but there was no one there. The senior boys said their supervisor chased an intruder away from the school. We couldn't sleep that night.

The Sunday service was always held in the main chapel out by Queen Street. I was a part of the service. A number of boys were selected to be part of the procession. We wore pure white gowns.

The rest of the students were sitting in the pews. The boys were on one side and the girls on the other side. The students had on their Sunday clothes: white shirts, black ties, and black pants for the boys, white dresses for the girls, and, of course, the black shiny shoes. The service started with a hymn. We stand at the entrance of the chapel. The lead boy carried the wooden cross between the boys and girls as the hymn started. We walked slowly to the front of the chapel. There was a bench for us to sit on after the hymn was sung. The school principal, who was also the priest, said "Be seated," and we all sat down as one. At first, I didn't realize that I was part of the choir.

I got booted out of the choir for a couple of reasons. For one thing, we had to remember the names of the three Hebrew men who were thrown into the furnace by the King of Babylon. They didn't burn because they believed in God. This made them special. At the time I couldn't remember their names – Shadrach, Meshach, and Abednego (which I pronounced "In-the-bed-we-go"). The other reason I was booted was because my voice was changing, and I couldn't hold a note. I wasn't castrated.

We were given sermons with many lessons about life and how to behave. This was way over our heads. One of our older cousins explained one of the lessons that was given by the priest. I never heard this part; or, if I did, I did not understand it. He explained that there was part of the sermon that said we should not fornicate with girls. This term was not in our vocabulary, or even in our realm of understanding. Our cousin told us what fornicating was, but we still didn't know what that meant.

We also heard stories from supervisors. One supervisor loved to tell stories. She was a large German woman with thick legs. She would come to our dormitory before we went to sleep. In Shingwauk we had bunk beds. One night she came in to visit and tell us a story. She always sat down on the bottom bunk. We all sat down on the floor in front of her and listened to her. One of our cousins, Walter-iban, got up to go to the bathroom. Our supervisor was not there at the time. Walter-iban came back from the bathroom and went behind the bed she sat on. He got down on his back and slid underneath the bunk bed. He slid until he could look up her skirt. It took everything we had not to laugh.

The juniors went to a public school called Anna McCrea. I started grade three there. It was situated across the open field from the main building. We walked to school every day. There was a huge woodlot to the right of the school, and we walked through it on the way there. We played in the woodlot after school and on the weekends.

I was the tallest kid in my grade three class. Every time we lined up in a row to walk down the hall, I slouched down to become smaller. I was always at the back of the line. I slouched everytime we walked down the hall. I slouched towards gym. One day we went outside to play baseball. At the end of the game, one of the boys refused to give the bat back to the teacher. The boy would not listen to the teacher. I could see that the teacher had a problem with the boy. I took control. I grabbed the bat away from the boy and gave the bat to the teacher. After that I slouched back to class with the rest of the students, at the back of the line.

I attracted a lot of attention from this incident. One of the girls in my class started to do projects with me. She had long and dark black hair. Everyone in our class liked her as she was friendly with everyone. I fell in love with her. It did not last long, though. She had bad breath and I had standards.

Several years later, while a student in grade five, I was transferred to grade six. I caught up to my older brother academically. He was bored of school and quit school the following year.

There was a winter carnival during sixth grade. The administrators built an outdoor hockey rink by the school. One of the events held there was a boys' skating race. Our cousin, Norman, qualified for the final race. There were a total of five skaters. They were to skate around the outside of the rink three times. We cheered loudly from the top banks of the snow piled up alongside the rink. Norman was leading at the final turn. He was skating very fast. His long red and white scarf was wrapped around his neck and it was flying straight out as he approached the finish line. It was like the scarf of the Red Baron, the famous World War I pilot. It slipped down to the ice and he stepped on it with his skate. He fell down and slid hard into the boards. He lost the race. It was a big letdown for us. I remember we did not talk to him for a long time after that.

The native students were all considered good skaters. I was the exception. I wobbled on my skates. I would get started down the ice and then try to scrape the top of the ice with my skate in order to stop. But what happened was I would take a huge gouge out of the ice. Then I would slowly pivot to come to a complete stop before I would skate back to where I started. It wasn't pretty but it worked for me!

The intermediate and senior boys were very good hockey players. They played in tournaments. The supervisors and the principal were the coaches. There was a big tournament for the boys to go to the finals. They were short one player. They needed to have a full team to play. They found out that I could skate; or that I could stand on skates. I was placed in the blue station wagon along with other students. The supervisor drove us to the game. We were all eager to play.

In the change room I was given the equipment. I didn't know how to put it on! The protective cup was on the outside of my hockey pants when I finished dressing. It was also upside down.

I looked like a medieval knight. Some of the other players on our team helped me to dress properly. I never played in a hockey game before. I barely knew how to skate. In the third period the referee told the coaches that all the boys had to play. The coach told me I was to take a shift. I at least stayed upright on the ice. The puck came to me as I was standing near the boards. An opposing player bodychecked me straight into the boards. I did not even touch the puck. I said "sorry, excuse me" to the player. I thought I got in his way.

Also during this first shift, our team was taking the puck up to the other side of the ice and I tried to follow. I was picking up steam as I neared centre ice. All of a sudden everyone was skating towards me going the other way. I stuck out my skate to stop but I spun out instead. I was still sliding towards the end boards when the other team scored. We lost the game. After the game, I did not sit with my teammates in the blue station wagon to return to Shingwauk. I ended up riding in the bed of a snow-covered truck. I was all by myself and it was cold. I sat there with my hockey stick and it started to snow. We stopped at a red light. I sat at the back looking gloomy. A man with his wife was behind us in a car. They waved to me and I waved back with the saddest wave ever. We continued ahead and they turned left.

That was the end of my hockey career. I joined the judo club. It was being offered by one of the supervisors. He had the local YMCA involved with the program. I became really good. The classes were held during the week at the residential school. Near the end of the term I was throwing the older boys around. We travelled to Camp Petawawa, a training ground for Canadian soldiers, for a judo tournament one spring. There were kids from everywhere. I had a yellow belt. I won my first couple of fights. There was this one non-native kid that I had to fight to get to the finals. I threw him down and I had him pinned down. The referee started the count.

The kid under me shouted "ouch!"; I let up a bit and he flipped me over. He won and went on to the next round. At the end of the season, the judo teachers gave me straw slippers with velvet green straps and the next level belt.

The other students didn't dare steal it.

CHAPTER 19

Osh-kih-zaa-gee-win
(Young love)

I was in grade six with older students when I started noticing girls. There was this one non-native girl in grade eight that all the boys liked. She was really nice and talked to everyone. When she talked to a native student, he thought he was in love, but she was just being nice. The non-native students did not like us talking to her, of course. There were some disagreements and there were some fights.

Her younger brother was in my class and we got along well. We became good friends at school. He even invited me to his birthday once. This made the residential school supervisors scramble for a birthday present for me to bring and proper clothes for me to wear. The day arrived and I walked to his house. I did not have a clue what a birthday party was. I remember we played games and ate cake. His parents were really nice. He asked me to come up to his bedroom. He had a new bicycle standing up against the wall there. I went to sit on it, and it crashed down to the floor. It created such a loud sound that his parents came rushing into the room. I was especially embarrassed when the older sister came into the room, too. I was never invited to his birthday party again.

One year we had a young teacher at Anna McCrea. It was to be her first year teaching and she was very eager for us to learn. But the native students were reluctant leaners. We always struggled with our subjects, from math to spelling and science. When reading time came, we fought our way to sit at the front. The teacher sat on a wooden chair to read us a story. We sat close to her on the floor. She always wore a dress or a skirt. We always sat up with our backs straight, looked up to her, and listened intently.

One of the girls in our class thought she was a horse. Every recess she would trot and prance around the school playground. Her long blonde hair was her mane. It flew with the wind as she ran around the yard. She would neigh and pound her foot into the ground. She even recruited other girls in the class into her herd. There was a full stable of them. She found some little colts follow her, too. We teased them a lot during recess. We got kicked in the shins if we got too close. She also bit some boys who were slow or foolish enough to get close to the herd. She acted like a horse and she had buck teeth like one.

We always took to the woods after school. It reminded us of home. We saw and heard the kih-chi-kaan-nay-sheen-shug (chickadees), moh-noh-gun-nay (brown and white woodpeckers), and the ad-tih-tah-moog (squirrels). They connected with us. During the weekends, we went up Queen Street to Bellevue Park. It was situated along the St Mary's River. We were able to see the white water upriver where the falls are. That reminded us of home, too. There were ni-ka (geese) everywhere. We looked at them and saw a great feast, but we knew we couldn't touch them. There were also buffalo in a closed area surrounded by a fence. We had only seen them in cowboy movies. We waved a red jacket at them, but they did not charge.

Back in Shingwauk we watched a lot of television. We had more choices now. We were moving away from westerns and *Bonanza*. *The Man from U.N.C.L.E.* with Napoleon Solo and Illya Kuryakin took over the school. They were two young and handsome heroes who always helped people in danger in the nick of time. They always got their man. They always got their woman, too. We liked this show because of the fast action and quick thinking of its heroes. After *The Man from U.N.C.L.E.* was over, we went to bed and I would start thinking about our predicament in residential school. I thought about how to get home. I hoped Solo and Kuryakin would save us.

We often fought the Cree, the Mush-kee-goog. It would be over a girl or just the fact that they thought the school was theirs since they were there first. We Ojibway thought we ran the joint. We actually did. Our cousin, Charlie, was at the centre of this battle. He was a scrapper; he still is.

Once we heard there was going to be a fight between Charlie and one of the Cree boys. At first, we were not allowed to go see the fight. Frank Beardy-iban stepped in and said that if anyone was going to stop us from going to the fight, they would have to go through him first. Nobody messed with Frank. He was the biggest Ojibway in the school. The fight was held behind a big boulder in the open field. The fight ended quickly with Charlie winning. The challenger eventually got up off the ground and said something in Cree to the other Cree students. They took a few steps towards Charlie. Just then Frank spoke up and told them that Charlie won and that if anyone went after him, they would have to deal with Frank. The thing about Charlie was that he was the wrestling champ in all the high schools in the area.

My brother Angus quit school after grade six. Many other students did not return to school that year, either. Instead they stayed home to help their parents hunt and fish and trap on their ancestral lands. My younger brother and some of our cousins stayed in school for a couple more years. They eventually quit school, too.

Slowly, my support system was leaving Shingwauk. As a result, the school administrators placed me in a home to live with a non-native family. They were Welsh, so I was introduced to the music of Tom Jones and the Beatles. I also had to start grade seven in a different elementary school.

The Indian Affairs agent moved me to another family, my third in only a few years. They treated me well. The father was a school principal, the mother stayed at home, and they had two daughters. I remember that he built a sauna in the basement. Their house was beautiful, but it was not for me. I left.

Fortunately, two of my cousins, Annie and Juanita, lived in the home of non-natives close by. We would meet up to go for walks through Bellevue Park. I received a new clothing allowance and we went to Woolworth's Department Store downtown to shop. It was the first time I shopped for clothes for myself. I bought the pants, then put them on in the store and went out to see my cousins. I felt good about my new look and walked with my head held high. I passed a young boy and his father out in their front yard. I heard the boy say "Look Dad!" as I walked by. The father quickly told the boy to be quiet. I walked a few blocks and checked my new pants. I then felt the huge paper tag still attached to the leg. I had forgotten to take it off.

Soon I was to enter high school and was enrolled in Sault Collegiate. I met only one other First Nations student there. He was in the senior grades. Oddly enough, the only subject I enjoyed was French. I was never a good student of French, but the teacher was nice to me. At this time my hair was getting long and kind of wavy, which made sense considering the times: it was the beginning of the hippy movement. Our gym teacher made a joke about my long hair and something to do with Chief Dan George, who starred in the film *Little Big Man*. The other students laughed. I turned red.

The remaining First Nations students hung out in the pool hall in downtown Sault Ste Marie. Our blue denim jackets always had the collar pulled up. Our cigarettes would dangle from our mouths. We shot pool. We thought we were cool. Others knew we were cool. On Saturdays we would shoot pool all afternoon. At four in the afternoon we rushed home. The non-natives would ask us, "Why are you in such a hurry?" We told them that we had to be back home by five to watch Bugs Bunny.

CHAPTER 20

Nih-gee-way
(I'm going home)

High school became a problem for me. I couldn't complete the work. I found it too difficult. I started drinking.

We would always seem to end up in a bar. We were underage and usually sneaked in near the end of last call. The only thing we could afford was draught beer. It only cost ten cents a glass.

I had long hair near the end of my high school years. I was very self-conscious; my legs were so skinny. I used to wear long underwear to make my legs look thicker during springtime.

Once I was invited to a house party. It was a house where there was a sign that said "Shoes Off or Fuck Off!" There were many people there with long hair with skinny bodies like me. I fit right in. One of these guys was seated at a table with his arm stretched out across it. I watched as he sunk a needle into his vein and pushed a liquid in. Then he stood up and shook his hair as he walked out into the living room. To me this was a way to prove to his friends that he was a man and needed to be respected. I left soon after that. The sign was more interesting to me.

Alcohol became a huge part of my life at this time. I started drinking heavily, but it only made me throw up in the end. I asked the Indian Affairs education agent to be transferred to the high school in Fort William, which is now Thunder Bay. My older sister Ruth lived there at the time. I was denied. Instead, the Indian Affairs agent moved me from the Welsh home to another home. My grades were failing. I was falling.

I had little money. I needed cash for my drinking. The money we received as a stipend for new clothes came through vouchers from Indian Affairs. I went downtown to Woolworth's to buy blue jeans. I shopped around and eventually found a pair of jeans that I liked. I bought them without trying them on first. When I returned home, I tried them on, but they didn't fit. I took them back to Woolworth's the next day and told the cashier that they did not fit. The cashier asked me if I wanted another pair of jeans or a cash refund. I asked for the cash. I did this a number of times. It was a good gig.

One night another student and I went out drinking. It was closing time at the bar and so we went to a nearby hotel to hang out. He said that if we knocked on some of the doors, we would find a lonely lady and she would take us in. We knocked on the doors and someone called security. They chased us and we went outside to the fire escape. One of the security people grabbed me by the collar of my winter coat. I was dangling in midair for a moment before he let me go. We ran in different directions. It was cold and it started snowing. The police chased me down, put me in cuffs, and I spent the night in jail. I went to court and the judge told me that I was to appear in court again at a later date. My friend was caught, too.

Our court date was set in the morning during the week. I arrived to the courthouse early so I decided to walk around the city. I started thinking about home. I started thinking about the land, the rivers, and the waterfalls. I spoke aloud the Anishinaabay names given to certain places such as Shoosh-koh-bih-kay-wih-nih-gahm (Smooth Rock Portage), I-kway-wih-nih-gahm (Woman's Portage), and Ish-pah-kway-yaa-wih-nih-gahm (Where the tall trees are).

The judge sentenced us to one day in jail. It was close to twelve noon when we arrived at the jail. The police officers left after we were booked. The jailer looked at us and said that he did not want to have to make us lunch, so he just let us walk. I was in and out of jail in less than an hour.

My friend said he was going back to school. I told him I was going home. We said good-bye and we never saw each other again. I started hitchhiking. I left everything I had and did not tell anyone where I was going. This was my escape. It was still winter. I had only the clothes I wore and a few dollars.

My first ride was with a middle-aged man who asked where I was headed. I told him that I wanted to go to Fort William and he said that he could not get there and back on his lunch hour. He dropped me off at the edge of town. My next ride was a mail lady. She drove me to the next town north of Sault Ste Marie. The town was called Hayden. The sun was setting.

I went into a variety store as there was another hitch hiker waiting for a ride along the highway. I bought a bottle of pop and a bag of chips. On my way out of the store, a man followed me and stopped by a Camaro. He asked me where I was going. I told him Fort William and he said to hop in. He was headed there too, and he wanted company. He was on his way to Winnipeg to attend to some business. His business was selling black lights. He took some pills to keep himself awake. We arrived in Fort William later that night. He dropped me off at a Greyhound bus station. I called my sister Ruth, and she came to pick me up. She was surprised to hear from me. I made it back to my family.

Epilogue

Looking back now, as an adult, I keep thinking back about my educational experience in the provincial school system; I think back about my formative years learning the Anishinaabay education system in our Anishinaabay language. Experiencing the two forms of education, the Anishinaabay and the provincial methods, I have come to a conclusion that will benefit the native and non-native societies.

The current educational system needs to change. One solution is to have all Anishinaabay communities use the original language. The Anishinaabay students are in the communities learning the oral language until they know how to listen, speak, and understand the language. Our oral Anishinaabay language has our curriculum in it.

For now, Anishinaabay adults in every community will need to learn the language. They could get paid for taking the language as compensation. To this day, and starting from the 1970s, the language has been taught to only the students in the elementary and high schools and in colleges and universities. For about sixty years the Anishinaabay language has been taught in the classrooms without producing a single fluent Anishinaabay speaker. There are speakers but they are second language speakers. There is not a single college or university that only teaches in the language with full-time Anishinaabay language speakers as full-fledged professors. These would be fluent Ojibway language speakers using the old Ojibway way of speaking.

Teaching the Anishinaabay language only to the children has produced an unbalanced force in the universe. The Anishinaabay parents had the power to teach in the language to their children. The children looked up to their parents and all their relations because the children wanted to be like their parents and community members. Now, in the present day, only the children learn the vocabulary in the classroom but there is no one to talk to at home or in the community as the adults do not speak the language. The children now hold the power of the language. Some parents resent this because they are now unable to communicate in their ancestral language to their children. It is hard to be an Anishinaabay today! Sun-nah-gun! (It is difficult!)

My observation to break this cycle of only teaching the children the language in the classroom is to start teaching the Anishinaabay adults in their communities the language. Let the children be present in the teaching of the language, in the traditional way of learning the language orally. Hire the remaining fluent Anishinaabay speakers to come and live in each Anishinaabay community. The adults and children are taught in the language until they become fluent speakers. The adults and children learn the language for ten years. After this the Ontario curriculum is introduced to all community members. The children receive the Ontario school curriculum and see how they progress through it. The adults can receive the adult education system.

I have seen this work first-hand. My older sister Ruth did not go to school until she was ten years old. She did not know a word of English when she started school. In grade thirteen she received the speech award for public speaking at her high school. One of her prizes was a blue bike that she brought back to Washi Lake. I also remember Ruth translating for Indian Affairs officials during treaty days on the reserve in Ogoki Post as the people did not understand a word of English.

My cousin Juanita married this smart Anishinaabay man. Danny was one of the first Anishinaabayg to enter the science program at Lakehead University. He was twelve years old when Indian Affairs found out he was living in the wilderness with his parents. Danny caught up with his cohorts and surpassed the other students in his class.

There are many other examples like this where Anishinaabayg did not start school until about ten years old. What they had was the Anishinaabay language and its system of knowledge. It was easy for them to learn the Ontario curriculum. Bring this change to the education system now! Besides, what are we going to be doing for the next 500 years!

This change will have economic benefits for the Anishinaabayg and Canadians. Jobs will be created to have institutions teaching in the Anishinaabay language. There will be social, education, political, law, and literature studies in the Anishinaabay language. Tah-min-noh-shin! (It will be beautiful!)

◆ ◆ ◆

I wrote this book to start a conversation about the state of the Anishinaabay language here on Turtle Island. The land and the Anishinaabay language operate in a spiritual manner. This book is about the Anishinaabay life before European contact. It is about the Anishinaabay life before the residential school program and it is about the hunting and gathering society of the Anishinaabayg.

The Anishinaabay and Canadian education systems have been experienced by my generation. I would like to see more Anishinaabayg write their stories so that other people can learn what we went through. I am presently teaching the Oneida GED program on Oneida of the Thames First Nations in southwestern Ontario. I have talked to my adult students about starting a writing program in their community. It would be great to have our Indigenous stories from our communities come out to record our point of view. It is kind of funny that here is an Ojibway teaching Oneidas in English.

There is so much to write about from our First Nations point of view. Our voices need to be heard by the next generation. It is like talking about our past in the present for the future generation. We can write about mistakes so that others can learn from our stories.

The next book I want to write is about what experiences I had in the world of the economy, in the world of education, in the world of politics, in the world of modern communications, and in the world of spirituality. I want to write about the future of the Anishinaabayg and our language. It is my dream, my vision, to have the Anishinaabay language be spoken in all our communities the way it was spoken before European contact. So, I say, pah-sih-kaa-taa (let's kick it)!

Amiiwepinaamaa.
(That is all for now.)
Miigwech.
(Thank you.)
Nindihzhinihkaaz Eli Baxter.
(My name is Eli Baxter.)
Nindohncihbaa Agohkiing.
(I come from Ogoki Post.)
Attick nihdohdem.
(Caribou is my Clan.)

Acknowledgments

I would like to acknowledge my parents, Gilbert and Barbara Baxter, who brought us up in the hunting and gathering society of the Anishinaabayg. They taught my brothers and sisters the Ojibwe language as our first language. My aunt and uncles also did the same thing in their families. This also goes to the Anishinaabay parents who sent their children to the residential schools. To all the survivors, this book is about us and how we move forward.

Miigwech! (Thank You!)

I would like to say Miigwech to Elizabeth and our two daughters for tolerating all my requests in dealing with the computer.

Matthew Ryan Smith was a great help in putting this book together. He listened to my ideas about First Nations issues and what I had to say about the Anishinaabay language. I talked to him about my experiences growing up in the last era of the Anishinaabay hunting and gathering society. Miigwech, Matthew.

Finally, I would like to acknowledge the people at McGill-Queen's University Press, especially Jacqueline Mason and Mark Abley for their attention and direction.

Index

Page numbers in italics refer to illustrations.

About the Author

Eli Baxter is an Ojibway language speaker. He was born in Washi Lake in Northern Ontario where his parents lived off the land as their ancestors did before European contact. He has two sisters and two brothers, along with various cousins who also know the Ojibway language.

They all grew up in their ancestral lands along the Albany River. At the age of seven the children were sent to residential school, first at Pelican Residential School near Sioux Lookout, Ontario, and then to Shingwauk Residential School in Sault Ste Marie, Ontario. All of the children retained their Ojibway language, but as adults they did not return to live in the hunting and gathering society and did not pass it on to their children.

Eli received his bachelor of arts degree from Lakehead University in Thunder Bay, Ontario; the only person in his family that made this academic achievement. Eli became a certified elementary school teacher and taught for over thirty years in First Nations communities. He taught various grades at Wabih-sihmong (Whitedog), Ontario, for seven years before teaching the Ojibway language for twenty years to children from kindergarten to grade eight at the Chippewas of the Thames First Nation just outside of London, Ontario. Eli also taught the

Algonquian Language and Culture course for seventeen years at Western University. Currently, he teaches the Oneida GED program in Oneida First Nation.

Eli lives in London, Ontario, with Elizabeth and their two daughters.